A Breath Away

A Story of love, loss and light

Jeanne Selander Miller

ISBN: 1469980843
ISBN 13: 9781469980843

A coward is incapable of exhibiting love; it is the prerogative of the brave

—Mohandas Gandhi

This book is written for the loves of my life

To my Mother and Dad-
who taught me how to love

To Fred-
who loved me in my entirety

To Cullen and Gillian-
my children,
whom I love with my whole being

To Susan-

my sister,
thank you for believing in me
you are the best

To David Hazard-
my friend and mentor
thank you for all your help
and the encouragement that
I needed to write this story

Frederick Duncan Miller
The Bravest Man I Know

If I have learned anything it is this-
Love bravely-
It is worth the risk

CHAPTER 1

The Invitation

There have been times in my life when the loneliness has been overwhelming, the repercussions resounding and pervasive. It is helpful to remember at these times of profound loneliness that once upon a time I was greatly loved . . .

❦

It has been said that it is darkest just before the dawn. This notion teased around in my brain as I walked to the parking deck at 6 PM. It looked just like this when I got here this morning. The days are shortest in December but the holidays infuse that season with light. It was a cold, grey and damp; February in Detroit complete with dirty old snow. I understand why bears hibernate. I pulled my coat closed at the collar and shook off a chill as I stepped into the elevator. It was empty. Looks like most folks had already left. I had missed all the daylight hours, again.

It had been a long week already and it was only Wednesday. Only the commute to endure and I'd be home. I could get out of here earlier but if I'm not on the highway before 5, the commute time doubles. I was a little early. The traffic on the entrance ramp was still backed up. Shit. I suppose I could sit in the car or sit at home. What's the difference? The car was cold; that was one. I turned up the heat and quickly turned off the fan. It still blew cold air.

I flicked on the radio: NPR. <u>All Things Considered</u>. I lost myself in the events of the day and arrived at home unaware of how I got there. I didn't care; at least I was home.

I walked into the apartment and the light on the answering machine was flashing wildly. I played back the messages. Linda had called twice. Damn it. I forgot I told her I'd go out. It seemed like a good idea at the time. I could just hear her, " You know you spend too many nights home alone. Are you going to get all wrapped in a blanket and read some silly book?" It sounded so enticing. I checked my watch. 7:05. Reluctantly, I called her back.

"Hey girl, where do you want to go and when?" I hoped she wanted to cancel.

She bubbled over. " I have a plan."

"Of course you do." I know her so well. I braced myself and sat on the couch, as I was certain she would elaborate.

She laughed. "Let's go to aerobics at Fitnesse and then out for a drink. Wherever you want. Promise."

"Is that the place in the 555 Building?" I droned.

She couldn't be serious? The 555 Building is located in Birmingham, where I grew up. But Birmingham was different in the 60's and 70's. Now it's Yuppie heaven where everyone is afflicted with *affluenza*.

"That's the one," she bubbled on.

"Seriously, I'm beat. Let's just grab a drink and call it an early night." I couldn't muster up any enthusiasm for this plan on my best day.

"Class starts at 7:30, Be There or Be Square." And she was gone. No discussion.

How many times am I going to let myself be manipulated into doing something I didn't want to do? I muttered and cursed at her. She had been talking me into participating in her plans since college. I pulled off my stockings and took note, good thing I shaved my legs this morning. I threw my suit on the bed. Great. The only clean leotard is light pink. Just like my skin. I'll look like a naked dancing woman. Why did I ever buy this color? Oh, that would be because it was on sale. I need to stop doing that. Questions asked, answered and a complete commentary ran through my head.

I left my apartment in a rush and got into my car. The internal chatter played on at full volume. I need to go to the car wash. I drag my ass out of bed everyday and go to work so I can have this beautiful life. I work month after month so I can make the car payments and still my car looks like crap. It's dirty and covered with road salt. What the hell is wrong with me? Other people I know, and actually like, care about these things. Why can't I

3

just go with it? I live in a world where people are defined by how they look, and what they do, where they live and what they drive, where they go and who they know. I feel so empty. This all seems so small and irrelevant. Is this the good life that I am working so hard to achieve? God help me if this is all there is.

When I arrived, Linda was in the lobby waiting for me. The florescent lights beamed brightly and Cindy Lauper crooned, "Girls Just Want to have Fun" through the stereo. The room was full of people in their twenties and thirties smartly attired in the height of 1980's dance wear, complete with matching leg warmers and sweat bands. Oh Dear God, what am I doing here? How is this my life? I signed in and paid the visitor's fee before I headed for the locker room to deposit my belongings.

Now this class was the antithesis of my ideal exercise class. If aerobics can be competitive then this was the class. Welcome to aerobics at Fitnesse. In an era of body beautiful and a collective attitude that reeked of –"I am more fit than you, look better in my leotard than you and in every way, shape and form says I am just better than you."

I was 26 years old and a bit of a Skinny Minnie at 5'6" weighing in at 114 pounds. I was totally intimidated by these aerobic divas.

The doors opened. The music of The Police beckoned and the waiting masses rushed into the studio to assure their position on the dance floor. I slipped into the back of the class. Not that it mattered because all four walls had been covered with floor to ceiling mirrors. There was nowhere to hide. I am not the world's greatest dancer. I have a tendency to step on toes, sometimes even my own. I always end up leading. Following along in this fast-paced dance class, where I did not know the routines, did not exactly help me to shine in my best possible light.

The minutes hung like hours as the group went right and I went left, and just when I got into step with the masses, the instructor gave a command, the masses followed and I was out of step yet again. I may not be a great athlete but I am a pretty good sport and over the years I have learned to laugh at my own ineptitude. Heaven knows I have had ample opportunity to practice. At the end of the class I was sitting on the floor, red faced in my pink leotard, panting and expressing gratitude that this particular exercise in humiliation had ended.

"Are you friends with Andrew Hardy?" I looked up and there was this tall, attractive man. He bent down next to me and looked me in the eyes.

Now, Andrew Hardy had been my philandering boyfriend for the last seven years and it only took me six years to gather up enough courage to break up with him. That was five months ago.

I looked into the face of this gorgeous man with sparkling eyes, a beautiful smile and a full beard. "I guess we're friends."

He launched into a full introduction. "My name is Fred Miller and I work with Andy at the Oakland County Prosecutor's Office. I remember meeting you at the Prosecutor's Christmas party at the Fox and Hounds."

I could not think straight. I was hot and still catching my breath. That party was over a year ago. I took this man's hand as he helped me to my feet and we left the aerobics studio.

5

I have no recollection if I said anything or even if I told him my name but I do remember waiting in the women's locker room. Cursing. Will I forever be associated with Andrew? What an asshole.

Linda peered out the door of the locker room. "I think that guy is waiting for you."

"No way." I looked at myself in the mirror. I was red faced. The interior monolog ran on. I look like I have been dragged behind the bus. Mom was right, redheads should not wear pink. "I'm not going out there."

We waited until he was gone before I consented to leave the locker room. To this day I cannot say for certain why I insisted on waiting. Was it my embarrassment with my inadequacy on the dance floor, my continued association with Andrew or just being shy and fearful of the attention of this very attractive man? What the hell is the matter with me? I am cautious with my heart.

I was pretty broken when my relationship with Andrew was over. It had been over for a long time. I kept trying to fix it. I wanted him to love only me, and that was never going to happen. In my heart of hearts I knew there was nothing at all to salvage.

I had spent years trying to cultivate and nourish an authentic relationship with Andrew. I now knew that he would never know me, see me or value the things that were important to me. I lived in a world where power, position, affluence and beauty were the currency of the day. If the truth be told, I had the wherewithal to compete in these arenas but the entire struggle and competition left me feeling empty and lonely. The question nagged at me relentlessly: is this all there is?

6

These last few months on my own had offered plenty of time for reflection. The conclusion being that if I was ever going to have a successful relationship I would need to enter it from a place of wholeness and to get comfortable being me. When Fred walked out the door that night I chastised myself for my cowardice and another lost opportunity.

Linda and I walked to a local bar and had a drink in town. I beat myself up in her presence and she added gasoline to the already blazing fire. "This cannot continue. You need to get on with the business of living and stop turning away from the opportunities that life is offering." She was right and I knew it.

On Saturday, the girls always had breakfast together. There were four of us and we had been doing this for years. It was our chance to catch up. It didn't matter what wonderful adventure you were involved with the night before, Saturday breakfast was with the girls. If you were in town the expectation was that you would be there, ten o'clock, no excuses.

Laughter is good for the soul and there was always plenty of laughter at Saturday breakfast. Linda shared with Patty and Nancy my major faux pas in letting this handsome man slip away, especially when it had the potential to offer up a double whammy because this guy was Hardy's boss. The girls affectionately refer to Andrew as AH as in asshole. Linda went on and on about how she had been going to aerobics for months and the first time I go that I am the one who meets someone, in spite of the pink leotard and the hoards of aerobic divas. The jury of my peers voted and concluded that once again

I am a fool. Only one option, I must return to aerobics with Linda that afternoon to seek out this mystery man. Really? I folded to peer pressure.

I would like to say that my return performance at aerobics was greatly improved but the sad fact of the matter was that I was equally as miserable as I had been the first time. But Fred was at the class and this time when he waited for me I did not hide from him. He chatted with Linda and I as we walked to our car. Oh dear, I am really attracted to him.

On Monday morning my assistant, Renee buzzed into my office. "Andrew Hardy is on the phone." Without pausing for breath she asked, "Do you want me to tell him you're busy?" She knows me so well.

"No, that's okay. I'll take it."

"Really? Okay." She was well aware of what I had been through and she tried to protect me from yet another bad decision.

The phone rang and I picked it up. "Hello."

He responded with his slow deep voice. It had been months since we had spoken with one another so we launched into the perfunctory inquisition about one another's well being. I tried to keep myself from caring and cut it short. "What can I do for you? I'm on my way out to a meeting."

"Oh, okay. Well there is this guy in my office, Fred Miller."

"Yeah, I've met him."

"He asked me for your phone number."

"You can give it to him." Asked and answered. I was direct so not to welcome any discussion.

"I know you have had trouble with stalkers, maybe I shouldn't give him your home number." How considerate. This may be the first ounce of consideration he had shown me in years.

"Okay, give him my office number." Problem diverted.

"I just wanted to be certain that you were okay. You know he is my boss and we work together." He wanted me to tell him not to give out my phone number. He clearly did not want me to date his boss.

"I don't have a problem with that. Really I have to go. Just give him my office number. Got to go. Bye."

I got off the phone. My heart was pounding and my palms were moist. Did that just happen? Life continues to surprise me. I wonder if he'll actually call. I hope he will.

I opened my office door and Renee looked at me with a raised eyebrow. She worked for me but she was also my friend. I gave her the bare bones synopsis. And she gave me a high five as I headed out to my meeting.

Later that afternoon Fred called. He wanted to take me to dinner but as it turned out I was going to a conference in Manhattan at the end of the week and we would both be away on vacations the following week. I would spend my vacation with my sister, Susan, in New York City and Fred was off to ski with friends in Colorado. We consulted our calendars. The earliest we could possibly get together was in three weeks on Friday, March 23.

9

I hesitated. I was returning from New York that morning but the real reason was that it would be my 27th birthday. He had plans on Saturday the 24th with his family. They had already rescheduled his brother's 19th birthday dinner because of Fred's vacation.

There was a lull in the conversation. One of us would need to acquiesce. It gave me a moment to consider the situation. I evaluated my options ...

I did not want to put this date off for a month....

However, what if the date was terrible? After all it is my birthday.

I don't have any plans for the day, yet. But, something will come together. I know I won't be sitting home.

I debated the pros and cons with myself and concluded: Oh, what the heck.

"Friday, the 23rd will be fine. I don't have any plans for my birthday. It will give me something to look forward to."

Little did I know how accepting this invitation would alter the course of my life. There were actually two invitations being extended here. One was being extended by Fred for dinner and one was extended from beyond. I had asked God to help me move beyond the life that I was living. I had asked for something more. In retrospect, I now see that this was the answer to that call for help. It came as an invitation to participate in the fullness of life. And blindly I accepted the invitation, totally unaware, at the time, of what I had just agreed to. Saying yes was simply an everyday act of faith.

I had been dating other people. It's not that I didn't date. I liked this man but I told myself not to over-think it. It's just a date, but it didn't feel like that.

Some people take stock of their lives and make resolutions on New Year's Day but I have always done that on my new year, on my birthday. This new year started out pretty well. Within the last year I got out of graduate school at the University of Michigan and landed a good job at the Detroit Medical Center, and I finally got rid of a philandering, inconsiderate boyfriend. I was in a pretty good place going into my 27th year. When I returned from two weeks in Manhattan I learned that I was being promoted from a Planning Assistant in Corporate Planning to the Administrative Coordinator in the Gerontology Program at the Detroit Medical Center. The type of work would change and it meant more money. I was pretty happy about this as I had been in my initial position for less than a year. My career was taking off.

My colleagues took me to lunch to celebrate my return. They missed me while I was gone and I missed them too. We celebrated my birthday, my promotion and caught up on what had happened in the two weeks I was gone. I was blessed to work with these people. We frequently worked 60 hour weeks and too infrequently got together socially. This lunch was an exception and we relaxed and enjoyed one another's company.

After work my girlfriends gathered and shared a bottle of wine in my apartment as I dressed for my date. They pawed through my closet and suggested some ridiculous ensembles. In the end I opted for a silk teal blouse, fitted black trousers in raw silk and a pair of strappy black heels. Dressed for a night on the town, a little bit sexy but not over the top. Repeatedly I told them that even if it was my birthday, it was still just a date. Yeah, yeah, yeah, they were having a hard time believing it too. They enjoyed harassing me and having fun at my expense. The time had come to send them on their way. My date should be here soon. We bid one another adieu and promised to meet in the morning for Saturday breakfast.

There was a knock on the door. Seven-thirty, right on time. I looked through the peephole. This was not the guy I had agreed to go out with. I looked again. Had the image been distorted by the lens in the door? It had been nearly a month since we last saw one another and in this time Fred had cut his hair, shaved off his beard and his face was tan from skiing in Colorado. I opened the door and he beamed a big broad smile as he handed me a single long stem white rose and wished me a happy birthday.

I melted. "Thank you. It is beautiful." I stepped back from the door as he crossed the threshold.

"As are you."

"Would you like a glass of wine?" I offered. The bottle was open from when the girls were here. I'd already tidied up and set out two clean glasses.

"I don't think we should linger too long as I've made dinner reservations for 8 in the city." He stood by the doorway with his coat on.

"Give me just a moment and I'll be ready." I took the rose into the kitchen, selected a bud vase from the cabinet and put the rose into some water. I placed the rose on the table. Fred held my black cashmere coat for me. I gathered my gloves and purse. His manners were impeccable and they were not wasted on me.

He made me feel at ease as we chattered on about this and that on the way to the restaurant. The reservations were at an old world Italian restaurant, The Roma Café, located in the Eastern Market.

"We have a special table set for you, Mr. Miller." An older Italian gentleman, formally attired, showed us to our table. Our table was in a dimly lit little alcove completely separated from the remainder of the dining room with red velvet curtains. It was carefully appointed with white table linens and bathed in candlelight.

I felt like I was in a movie as the waiter unfolded the napkin and placed it on my lap and then did the same for Fred. He filled the water glasses, offered Fred the wine list and bowed gracefully as he backed away from the table.

"Do you dine here often?" I asked.

Fred smiled. "No, actually I've never been here before. I did make a few phone calls. I wanted it to be nice for your birthday." He had considered and attended to the details.

We discussed the wine list and what we intended to order for dinner. Fred ordered a glass for each of us and offered a toast to me on my birthday. We drank to health and happiness. He was well spoken and very much a gentleman. We began to relax into the evening. He made me laugh and smile. We discussed the mundane and the important with equal ease. We talked about our lives, our careers, our families, past hurts, present challenges and that which we hold dear. When I spoke he listened and he heard me. He was fully present and actively engaged in the moment. I felt as if I was the most important person on the planet.

The evening passed quickly as we learned about one another. He talked about his divorce and his ex-wife. He did not blame her. He felt that they were just poorly suited to one another.

He talked about his father and his alcohol use. Fred had made a very conscious choice and never drank more than two drinks a night. He didn't want to go down the same path his father did. I counted my drinks and took note to slow down a bit. I was already one glass ahead of him before he arrived.

I cannot remember what I had for dinner except that it was delicious. I do remember feeling star struck in the presence of this man.

"It's still early. Would you like to go dancing?"

He paid the bill and we went to Alvin's. The band covered all the hits of the time. We danced every song and I was filled with joy and laughter. This guy knows how to have a good time. We closed the bar at 2 AM and he took me home.

This was more than just a date. I really liked him. I asked him in for a cup of tea and he accepted. We lingered long over the cup of tea and shortly before dawn he left for home.

I pulled my clothes off and left them in a pile on the floor. They would need to go to the cleaners after a night of dancing. I crawled into the warmth of my bed. I pulled the quilt up around my shoulders. It had been an amazing day and although exhausted, I did not fall immediately to sleep. I was lost in the memories of the day and the evening. It had been years since I had not been kissed on my birthday. Fred left without a kiss good-bye. I lay awake and wondered if I was the only one who thought this was a magical evening. He was 33 years old, soon to be 34. Seven years older than me.

I asked myself:

Is he too old for me? I think not.

Is he my type? Oh, he was definitely my type-warm, personable, funny, smart… and sexy.

There was something about him…. we had really connected. It had been a long time since I had met someone who really listened and had something important to say and did so without imposing their views on me. Fred was interesting and interested. I wandered around in my thoughts for a while…. and the next thing I knew the phone was ringing.

I had forgotten about breakfast with the girls. "Sorry! I'm on my way."

After breakfast I spent the afternoon running errands, and over and over again my thoughts returned to Fred. In fact I thought about nothing but Fred.

That Saturday night I had dinner with Mom and Dad and Grandma. We celebrated my birthday in the dining room. Mom had made salmon with a dill sauce, broccoli, and baked potato, and of course Gram had made her specialty: an angel food cake.

My brother John lived in Boston and my sister Susan was in New York. They both called to wish me a happy birthday.

Birthdays are always a reason for celebration in my parents' home. It is a day to give thanks and celebrate the people in our lives. My parents are an absolute blessing to me. It is amazing, growing up in the affluent community that we did, that they were able to stay grounded and keep us grounded.

After dinner I helped Mom with the dishes. She washed and I put the dishes in the dishwasher. This was our bonding time in the kitchen. She asked about my date. I told her where we went and what we did and then I told her that Fred was divorced. She turned and looked at me, "You are *not* going to see him again…are you?"

I knew this would be hard for her. Both of my parents were raised in traditional Catholic homes. I, of course, was also raised Catholic….but I was not exactly a hard-line traditionalist.

I looked Mom in the eye and reached to take her hands in mine. "Will I see him again? . . . Only if he asks me."

There are many rules, spoken and unspoken, that practicing Catholics abide by. I have long considered myself an *ala carte* Catholic, often to the chagrin of the more conservative. I take the parts that work for me and say no thank you to the rest. I try to differentiate between God's rules and Man's rules. Sometimes that is difficult. I know this conversation was hard on Mom and I wouldn't hurt her for the world. This was not the time or place for this discussion and we both let it go and we enjoyed the remainder of the evening. I was beat so I went home early. The night before had been a late one.

After a wonderful evening, as I drove back to my apartment, I considered why my path had diverged from my traditional Catholic upbringing. Perhaps it was the byproduct of my education and my travels that had broadened my view of the world, and exposed me to diverse people and the wisdom garnered from a wide variety of spiritual traditions.

What I did not consider, as there was no way of knowing, was that life itself was about to issue me an invitation.

I was about to be invited out on a journey that would lead to the heights and depths of love . . . and to places of the spirit that I would need incredible faith and courage to travel.

Places where this world and the next touch and transform each other.

As I undressed and slipped into bed, the only invitation I was interested in was another one from this intriguing man I had just met.

CHAPTER 2

Love is a Verb

On Sunday, March 25, while I was giving a bridal shower, Fred called and left a message on my answering machine, "Hi, it is a beautiful spring day, would you like to go for a walk?"

I took the messages off the machine. "Missed opportunity." I was glad he called.

He called again later in the week and we made a date for Friday night.

Friday was Good Friday and Fred had acquired tickets for the Detroit Symphony Orchestra. The Pastor of Christ Church and the symphony were doing a combined lecture and performance of musical selections by Hayden on <u>The Last Words of Christ.</u> This was not an average second date and this was not an average man.

The First Word-*Father, forgive them, for they know not what they do.*
The Second Word-*I assure you, today you will be with me in Paradise.*
The Third Word-*Dear woman, here is your son.*
The Forth Word-*My God, my God, why have you abandoned me?*
The Fifth Word-*I am thirsty.*
The Sixth Word-*I am finished*
The Seventh Word-*Father, into your hands I commend my spirit.*
-The Gospels of Matthew, Mark, Luke and John

We sat and listened and Fred held my hand with great tenderness. The symphony played and Orchestra Hall was filled with music. The minister spoke and I thought about the Passion of Christ and reflected on the words.

Forgive them for they know not what they do.

The words echoed around in my head. Collectively we need forgiveness for the hurts we consciously or unconsciously inflict on others. Is there an unspoken understanding developing between Fred and I? Are we letting go of past hurt and beginning to open up to life and love? Perhaps this man who holds my hand shares my belief that the purpose of life is to make one's way back to The Source and that life itself is a spiritual journey.

So many of the people are not conscious of this. I do not want to live my life like that. I want to wake up to what life has to offer me and to be aware of all the beauty that surrounds me. My head tells me to proceed with caution. My heart says otherwise. What kind of man is this? Have I met my soul mate? Is this man and this relationship the key to unlocking the authentic life that I have been searching for? I keep my thoughts to myself lest I frighten my new friend.

The romance unfolded and over the course of the next few weeks we began to open up our hearts. We saw each other nearly every day and rarely left without a plan to be together again. The relationship progressed rapidly. The winter gave way to spring and the days lengthened and grew warmer.

One sunny afternoon in April there was a knock on my door. When I answered Fred handed me a huge bouquet of spring flowers. He had cut every flower from his garden. There were daffodils, tulips, hyacinths and irises. They were abundant, fragrant and beautiful. The flowers in this bouquet were grown and selected with love.

Fred's day-to-day demeanor reflected his thoughtfulness and I was blown away by the generosity of his heart. His thoughtfulness and generosity were not saved for special occasions but were gifts freely given daily.

He was resistant to calling what we were feeling love. "I have used that word before and so wrongly; before I use it again, I want to be certain."

I had been "in love" before, complete with lies and betrayals. I understood his hesitancy. But this looked like love and felt like love. Could this be the real deal? I kept my own counsel and practiced patience as our feelings began to take root and anchor us to one another.

In early May I was invited to Ellen's wedding and I brought Fred as my date.

I grew up next door to Ellen and she is two years my junior. Her sister, Sara, is my age and Ellen is my sister's age. The four of us spent a great deal of time together during our childhood. Sara is married and has a daughter and was pregnant with her second child. It was not lost on me that even my younger sister's friends were getting married. I did not think of myself as an old maid but apparently others felt free to comment on how I was still single. I braced myself for the intrusion by my well-meaning neighbors into the status of my love life.

"Twenty seven years old and still single?"

"When I was your age I already had three kids."

"I can't believe that a beautiful girl like you is still single."

Blah, blah, blah, the unsolicited commentary continued.

I bit my tongue and smiled. I hoped Fred could endure.

This was the first time Fred would meet Mom and Dad. We slipped into the pew next to them. Mom leaned over and whispered in my ear. "He has great hair." Fred's hair was curly brown with natural highlights. She smiled as if to give me her approval.

We were seated with my parents at the reception. Fred was charming and Mom was charmed. She really did not want to like him because he was divorced, but in spite of everything she was disarmed and taken in by his grace and charm. Dad was more accepting. He and Fred hit it off from the start.

My worry about the evening had been for naught. I told myself to give it up as I so often worry about things and create imaginary problems that never materialize. Worry is a lack of trust and I needed to trust this man. He certainly could handle himself without my relentless fretting.

As we said our good-byes and headed out the door of the reception, Ellen called my name. "Jeanne." I turned in her direction and she threw me the bouquet like she was handing off a football. All I could do was laugh. Fred laughed too. The joy on our faces was apparent to all.

Mom plays by the rules of the church. I have a tendency to follow my heart and hope that God will understand. In my heart I know that Freddy is a child of God and delights the hearts of all who know him. How can this be wrong? I just did not believe it was. Mom tried to work around it and looked for a loophole in the church law. I did not care. It did not worry me. If God will forgive all things, certainly he can forgive someone whose marriage just didn't work out. People make mistakes. Making mistakes is part of the human condition.

This man is the answer to the unspoken longing of my heart. He is a gift of The Creator and I decided that I would not make the mistake of missing out on what had been given because the gift did not conform to someone else's rules.

I have long been on a spiritual journey. Sometimes I am on the path and sometimes I am far afield. It is often easier when I keep company with those who are conscious of the journey and the path. I believe there are many paths and the paths may differ. I have friends who are comfortable with traditional Christian religions and, although some of it rings true in my heart, there is much that I cannot embrace. I have a gut level feeling that this is not the path that God intends for me. What is my path? I struggle. I have a tendency to gravitate towards the sinners or at least the less pious. They are more welcoming of my idiosyncrasies and I feel less judged. If the truth be told they're just more fun.

I seek to find a way that allows me to be myself, as I have been created to be, and still find a way to live in the love of God. I find it completely incomprehensible that I cannot do both. When I contemplate The Source of all creation, The Infinite, I am awestruck. Traditional religions offer answers to all questions. I cannot abide with this, as only The Source is all knowing. I struggle and the struggle is difficult for me to articulate but I think Fred understood. Time would tell.

As I reflect back on my love affair with Fred, I could try and sanitize the past and gloss over the sexual chemistry, and focus only on the spiritual connection that Fred and I had for one another, but that would give this love story short shrift. The truth is that we could not keep our hands off of one another. Fred was a fabulous lover from the first time when we made love on my living room floor, and my Siamese cat made a nest on Fred's sport coat where it was dropped on the floor and my lavender silk dress and panties lay just inside the doorway where I had been freed of them. Other people's moral code may demand chastity. But that was the furthest thing from my mind. I could not help myself, nor did I want to. Call it passion, call it lust, call it love, call it anything you want, just don't call it off. We lacked discretion and self-control when it came to one another. He was my vice and I was his. He was playful and fun and we took great pleasure and delight in pleasing one another and sex became another way that we connected.

And so all aspects of the relationship seemed to push me beyond the bounds of my carefully-scripted life. Early on Fred would quote Bruce Springsteen to say, "Can't start a fire without a spark." And so the sparks flew and we made love like a house on fire from early on in our relationship . . .

One weekend, after we had been dating for a couple of months, we were invited to Fred's parents' home for a picnic. Fred's parents lived in a large house in Bloomfield Hills with a swimming pool and a poolside cabana. The house and pool had fallen into a bit of disrepair as his parents had grown older and their financial circumstances had taken a turn for the worse. The cement around the pool had heaved and shifted over the years. The wooden trim could use a coat of paint and the gardens were over-grown.

Fred's mom, Mary Kaye, was warm and welcoming to me but her initial demeanor was a bit formal. Fred was 34 years old and I understood that I was not the first woman he had brought home to meet his family. Fred was engaging and jovial with his family as he and I helped his mother carry the food and drinks poolside.

She was friendly and made an effort to make me feel comfortable as she asked me about myself.

Don, his dad, sat in the cabana. He was waited on and deferred to by his wife and children. He was distant to me and appeared uninterested in meeting me. Fred loves his dad but their relationship had been strained for a long time, and I knew this. Don chain smoked and drank to excess. He was already intoxicated by mid-afternoon. In the past Fred had confronted his Dad about his drinking but to no avail. This had only served to alienate him from his father. The tension between them was palpable. He treated me with a modicum of courtesy but it felt perfunctory and not genuine.

Fred's sister, Shelley, and her husband Joel, were friendly. They obviously love Fred and they told jokes at his expense. He responded with the good humor I had grown to expect. They seemed a bit uncertain about me; they sat back and watched, reserving judgment until they knew me better. Fred had been hurt before and they didn't want to see him hurt again. I felt that they were courteous but cautious; for all they knew before they would see Fred again, I may be discarded and as irrelevant as yesterday's news.

◌

We visited my Grandmother about once a week. She had an apartment down the street from the aerobic studio where Fred and I had met. Gram is my hero and Fred knew this. I told him about her on one of our first dates. We were talking about what it meant to live a successful life. I told him that from my perspective my Grandma had lived an amazingly successful life. She did not graduate from high school because she was the oldest of seven children and money was in short supply. She never had a big important job. She did not have a great marriage. However, she was very wise, smart, hard working and loved life. She had people in her life that loved her. She made me laugh and I felt joy when I was with her.

Gram had an ability to see things clearly. She could cut through the extraneous and see to the heart of the matter. When we visited she always made the time to be with me. She had an unhurried way that made me feel valued. I loved to be in her presence and I benefited greatly from her guidance and wisdom. I loved her. I had explained this to Fred and he wanted to know her too. They quickly came to love one another.

Fred and I went to breakfast one Sunday morning in May. It was Mother's Day and it was snowing. The weather in Michigan is unpredictable but snow on Mother's Day left us sputtering about the need for warmth as we admonished ourselves for believing in the promise of spring and having had the audacity of putting away our winter clothes. We snuggled in close to one another on the same side of the booth as we attempted to stay warm. Fred put his arm around my shoulder and pulled me close to him as he tried to warm me. There was a powerful intimacy between us.

"I'm in trouble," Fred whispered in my ear as we waited for our hot tea.

" I know. Me too," I whispered back.

He continued, "I did not think this would ever happen to me. I thought I had lost my opportunity to ever feel like this. I feel like the love interest in a romance novel. But this is my life. I hate to talk about what is happening here for fear the magic will dissipate like the fog on a sunny morning."

I sat quietly and listened as he alluded to his feelings toward me. He hesitated. "Either this is going to work out for us, or one of us is going to be terribly hurt."

We spoke in generic terms about the risks of opening up one's heart and the risks associated with keeping it closed and safe. We concluded that it was already far too late to opt for safety. Love is risky.

I moved in closer and felt the strength and warmth of his body as he held me close. I know my heart was vulnerable and I was falling for this man. I thought about where my life had been. I know I had been waiting all my life to feel like this and now I was exhilarated at the prospect of what might happen next, but I was also afraid. What if this love turned out like the last one? What if I got hurt and broken again? Life and love are risky and require courage. Was I sufficiently healed? Was I strong enough to try again? This was the moment I decided to let go of fear and embrace the present.

The weather in Michigan improved and spring gave way to summer. It was an early Friday evening and I was home, after work, packing up a few things to go out to Fred's for the weekend when there was a knock on my apartment door. Before I could answer the door, in walked Andrew Hardy, my ex boyfriend, unannounced and uninvited. He approached to kiss me. I turned my head and he kissed my cheek. Standing back he looked me over. I was dressed in a little cardigan over a summer camisole. He moved my sweater aside to get a better look at my body and gave his approval, "You look really good."

I was pissed. He treated me like a piece of meat. He delayed me with his idle banter and my anxiety was building. I had not seen him since the fall. I can't believe he was so bold as to arrive at my apartment without being invited. I wanted him to leave.

"Let me take you out to dinner." He asked in his cavalier manner that I once found charming. I now knew him. He was insincere and an expert in the well-practiced art of schmoozing.

"Right here, right now? It is Friday night. I have plans." I spat the words out. Who did he think he was, waltzing in here and expecting me to be available to him?

"Cancel them." He gave me a sultry smile as he stepped into my personal space and put his hand on my hip. This was a gesture of familiarity and ownership. I was incensed.

"Do you know who I am seeing?" I stepped away from him and looked him in the eyes. I could not believe the gall of this man.

"Yeah, I know and I don't care. It doesn't bother me all that much. Look Baby, we have history together and we belong together and you know it. I thought you would be through with him by now." He was smug and full of self-confidence.

I loathe him and his arrogance. "You need to go. I have somewhere I need to be."

He looked at my overnight bag and laughed, "You know it is only a matter of time. I can wait." He walked out the door and I heard him snicker. He knew that he had upset me and that pleased him.

I called Fred in tears. "Hi…I'm sorry I am late." He knew I had been crying. The evidence was in my voice.

"Is everything okay?" His voice radiated concern.

"Andrew was just here." The tears kept coming as I tried to get myself under control. "I don't know why he still upsets me… he just does."

Fred paused. I waited for a response. "I don't understand." My crying confused him, as we had discussed Andrew and his betrayal ad infinitum. "Do you want to see him again? Do you still have unfinished business that you need to resolve?" I was crying harder now.

"I understand. Really I do. Do you need to try again with him? I'll be okay. You do what you need to do." He was letting me go. I could hear the sadness in his voice.

"No! For God's sake no! If you care anything for me at all, please, you would not want this for me. He made me miserable for years. I only want to be with you."

I could hardly get the words out. I had spent 7 years with a man who did not know me. Did not love me. And now the man I love was offering to walk away from this burgeoning love affair. I could hardly breathe at the prospect of the unraveling of my life.

"I'm so sorry, I did not understand. Please come over, darling. I'm waiting." There was tenderness and compassion in his voice.

"I'm on my way." I grabbed my bag and headed for the car.

30

Forty minutes later I arrived at Fred's house. It was now about 7:00 PM but there was still another 2 hours of day light on this perfect June evening. He had left me a note on the kitchen counter to meet him at the dock. I left my things and walked down the stairs towards the lake. The antique wooden sailboat was rigged and waiting at the dock for a sunset sail. There was an unspoken understanding between us. This was an unacknowledged hurdle. This encounter had closed the door on my past. I thought I had closed it long ago. The differences between these two men could not have been clearer. I closed the door on a past love for the final time. My new love was waiting. Fred had packed us a picnic and a bottle of wine. We sailed to the far side of the lake, and as the sun began to set, we raised our glasses to the beauty of the day.

The romance continued as we introduced one another to the significant people in our lives. The reception was warm and inviting for both of us. The weekends came and if we allowed it, we could be booked all weekend every weekend with family and friends. We guarded our precious time together and grew closer with each passing day.

Valentine's Day 1985

A bouquet of a dozen long stem red roses was delivered to my office. Fred had made reservations for us to have dinner at a fancy restaurant called The Money Tree. It was located in the Bank Building in the city. When we were together we filled our time with joyful chatter about the day's events or the people that we knew or any little thing that had happened since we had seen one another. This night was no different. I thanked Fred for the lovely flowers. We had wine and an extravagant dinner.

After dinner the waiter brought a tray of desserts for us to choose from. I chose one and Fred chose another. When the waiter returned from the kitchen, we continued our chatter as the waiter set our selections in front of us. Fred had asked me something and I respond in words he had told me about trial work, "A good attorney doesn't ask a question he doesn't already know the answer to."

Fred started to laugh.

"What?" I asked and then stopped speaking as I looked into his eyes.

He looked across the table at my dessert and I followed his gaze. The cake had been embellished with pastel flowers made of frosting and the words . . . Marry Me?

The answer is yes. Yes to love. Yes to life and yes to marriage to Fred.

And so, I had found love and a loving partner . . . someone who was perfectly suited to me . . . someone to accompany on the journey that was unfolding before us.

CHAPTER 3

Grace

Once we had made the decision to marry we opted for a brief engagement. We were only engaged for three months. We did get a bit of flack for this. How can you possibly plan a wedding in three months? I guess the simple answer would be that we just wanted to be together. Fred and I were soul mates. He was the answer to my heart's longing to love and be loved. There was not an earthly reason to delay.

The wedding would be an external sign to our families and friends of our commitment to a married life together but it was also, and more importantly, the binding of our souls to one another. It was the beginning of a journey we would travel together where our individual paths would intertwine.

⁓

Fred and I were married on May 11, 1985. The ceremony took place outdoors in a gazebo. It was a beautiful spring day in Michigan: 80 degrees and sunny. The spring flowers were in bloom and the apple trees were all in flower. It was the picture-perfect spring day.

Our families and friends joined us in the garden for the ceremony.

The music from the violin changed and signaled it was time. Dad leaned in to kiss me and started to say, "Jeanne Marie, you look so beautiful today and I want you to know what a wonderful daughter you are and…." He paused as he was getting choked up. I could hear it in his voice.

My eyes began to well up with tears. I looked up at my tall Nordic father, "Dad, not now." I knew if he continued that we would both cry.

Dad nodded. I took my father's arm as we started down the walkway to the gazebo where Fred was waiting. I took a moment and reflected on my good fortune: I have parents that love me. I have known this every day of my life. Some love stories are built in the day-to-day ways we live our lives and need no words.

When we arrived at the gazebo, Dad placed my hand in Fred's. Together we climbed the steps into the gazebo and were followed by our younger siblings, who were our attendants. The minister was waiting. Fred and I had chosen the readings, written our own vows and the blessing for the rings.

We struggled with the idea that the commitment we were making to one another would be bound by time and place. Instead, in our vows, we promised to love and honor one another always. The blessing of the rings spoke of the unbroken circle of love, a love that is unending and eternal and thus the inscription I had engraved in Fred's wedding ring was simply– Love Always. As we began this journey together we already understood that true love endures and is eternal.

At the conclusion of the wedding ceremony, Fred- my husband- lifted me up and off my feet to kiss me! Our guests cheered as they watched the sweet and tender exchange of our wedding kiss, and my feet were 8 inches off the ground.

There are times in life when joy comes to us in the purest form. When it is not tinged with fear or worry or sadness. These are the moments that we cling to. We embrace the present and we believe that there is nothing that can or will ever diminish this unbridled joy.

∽

Fred and I left the next morning for a three-week honeymoon in Italy and Greece. Other than plane reservations we were traveling without an itinerary. We would make it up as we went along.

This was our adventure and we were open to where it might lead us.

We arrived in Athens and decided to take a two and a half hour bus ride to Delphi where we spent the first night. The Temple of Delphi was built for the veneration of Gaia or mother earth, and Apollo, the God of prophesy, music, intellectual pursuits and healing.

Delphi is located in the mountains and is breathtakingly beautiful. We hiked and toured the area with a guide who explained that in ancient Greece, Delphi was considered the center of the world.

We learned that the omphalos or naval is an opening in the earth over a Castalian hot spring from which vapors rise. This is the location of the Oracle of Delphi and was considered the holiest of places in the ancient world. Pythia was the name given to the priestess of the oracle, and this position was always bestowed on an older woman, who sat on a tri-pod stool over this opening in the earth. She would go into a trance after breathing the fumes from the earth and then would prophesy.

The guide informed us, "Pythia was arguably the most powerful woman in the ancient world. Her prophecies were amazingly accurate and thus the Oracle of Delphi was consulted by many of the most powerful rulers for over 14 centuries."

After the tour we walked into town for lunch. Fred held my hand as we walked in companionable silence. Each of us was lost in our own thoughts. We sat at a small table at a sidewalk café. The pretty dark-eyed waitress took our order and returned quickly with our drinks, a salad, olives, yoghurt and bread.

Fred began, "I know that you don't believe in coincidence and neither do I." We had spoke of this before. I waited as he pondered and chose his next words carefully before speaking. Where was he going with this? I waited as he tried to sort it out for himself.

"Do you think it is possible that Pythia could predict the future?" He asked with hesitancy in his voice.

"Statistically accurate for over 14 centuries." I reiterated the words of our guide and then proceeded with my own. "It may be one thing if one woman was accurate in predicting the future over the course of her lifetime but there were different women assuming the role of Pythia and the predictions were accurate over the centuries. What is the likelihood of that?" I tried to put this into a scientific analysis and wrap my head around the possibility. "There would be so many uncontrolled variables."

"Just because it does not qualify as good science, does that make it any less valid?" "What was the Source of the visions? How could these prophecies be so accurate?" He asked gently as we explored our own thoughts and feelings about the prophecies.

"I don't know how to explain what I am feeling exactly. I had a very real sense of being in a sacred and holy place." I proceeded slowly as these notions took root and I attempted to find the words.

"Does that sound crazy?" I asked.

"No, not crazy at all, I felt it too." Fred paused and in doing so allowed space for me to continue.

I felt at ease and accepted and so I continued to piece together what I was thinking. "If God would speak to Moses through a burning bush, is it not possible that sacred prophecies and visions could have been given to the Greeks at Delphi?" I waited for reassurance.

Fred nodded to me, "Go on."

"The ancient Greeks taught us about democracy, philosophy, biology, mathematics and physics. The scholars of the time included Plato, Socrates, Pythagoras and Aristotle. In modern times we give this work and the scholars their due and yet dismiss their take on the spiritual world. I have a sense that the ancients understood something that we no longer do."

I paused and looked into Fred's eyes. Was all of this spiritual talk making him uncomfortable? "All I can say at this point is…. I just don't know."

"Neither do I. But I have a sense that there may be something going on that I can't pretend to understand."

This conversation laid the groundwork for a new level of spiritual exploration.

I loved that Fred was willing to remain open to possibility. He was willing to consider the spiritual without being bound by rules, doctrines or other prefabricated answers. This kind of thinking about pre-Christian prophecy was way out of bounds from both of our traditional upbringings. It was the kind of thinking that most of the people that we associated with would easily dismiss but we did not.

"I believe that there may be many truths that lie beyond that which is scientifically verifiable today, the operative word being today." Fred said as he finished the last of his salad.

"My understanding of so many things is limited and that clearly does not negate their existence," I said.

I felt an immense freedom to be able to talk about my spiritual inquiry with Fred, for so long I had kept this all to myself. The fact that Fred was open to a spiritual exploration was a huge relief. He prodded me intellectually and we asked questions that pushed us further down the path.

"So," he asked, "are you suggesting that the spiritual world may exist right alongside of this physical world we inhabit? Do you think it is possible that the ancient prophesies of Pythia were given to help us see beyond the limits of this physical world?"

"You are asking me? Remember I haven't a clue," I laughed, " but for the sake of argument let us suppose that the prophesy of Pythia was indeed a communication with the spirit world. If that is the case, is it not possible that there are modern-day prophets that still interact with the spiritual world? Do we dismiss them as mentally ill, misguided or charlatans?" I answered Fred's questions with more questions of my own.

When we had finished our lunch, Fred and I had come to the same conclusion, we just didn't know. Fred laughed as he reached across the table and took my hand, "We don't even know what we don't know."

We left the café and walked to the Pythian Stadium. The Pythian Games were held in 582 BCE and were the precursor to the modern Olympic Games. I wandered through the stadium; it was quiet, as there were only a handful of visitors that day. The sun had burned away the clouds of the morning and it was delightfully warm. It was easy to let my mind wander and think of the athletes from ancient times who gathered here to compete. I turned my head and saw that Fred was down on the field.

As I watched, he crouched down as if a runner at the starting line, and then he ran the length of the stadium field. He was tall and lean and strong. He ran with speed and grace. As he crossed the imaginary finish line he raised his arms above his head in a gesture of the victorious.

The other visitors paused and looked in Fred's direction. He smiled and beamed at me as we clapped and cheered for him. The games were given human form. The visitors enjoyed the show. "Yeah! Good for you!" "Well done."

When Fred stepped off the field, he was the embodiment of joy. "You are such a strong and beautiful runner. It was awe-inspiring just to watch," I said.

Fred was breathing hard after the run. "I just wanted to know how it felt. I just could not let the opportunity pass. I needed to run here."

He paused to catch his breath as I wrapped my arm around his waist. I felt the strength and warmth of his body as I held him close to me. It felt like I was connected to the essence of the man, to his life force. He just radiated his abundant enthusiasm for life and for this moment.

Later in town, people would stop us on the street and ask if he was the man who was running in the stadium. They laughed and joked with us.

From that moment I knew: Fred was the kind of person who did what others want to do, except they hold back for fear of judgment. As Fred beamed and chatted with these new found acquaintances, I could see that he was confident and pleased that his afternoon run had freed people to feel comfortable and at ease in his presence.

I realized, there on the ancient streets of Delphi, that there was *something* about Fred- something in his spirit that was light and free. When I was with him – that lightness of his being was contagious—I felt it and others felt it too ...what was it?

Freer to be my authentic self.

Fred finished talking with all of his admirers and took my arm as we walked away. I smiled to myself as I wondered: was meeting Fred and falling in love, just my good fortune, or was it some kind of Divine providence? Either way…I'll take it.

When we left Delphi and traveled to Athens, we chose to visit all the archeological sites in a quest to know what the lives of our predecessors were like. Were they so different from us? I don't think so. What did they know? What did they have to teach us?

In the back of my mind, a question emerged. Was there something we were supposed to learn from the ancients?

∽

Okay. We were on our honeymoon, this was not a spiritual retreat. We were really interested in having a good time, and our attention shifted to pleasure, laughter, great food and wine.

One evening we walked into Athena's, in the shadows of the Acropolis, to taste the local cuisine, enjoy some wine and partake in some general frivolity. We were seated in an open-air courtyard under a portico at the edge of the dance floor. The evening was warm and the gentle Aegean breeze blew in my hair.

"Good evening. My name is Constantine and I will be your server tonight. I welcome you to my city and to Athena's." Our server was gracious and engaging, as he looked us both in the eyes before dropping his head in a gesture of humility.

" Thank you Constantine. This is Jeanne... my new bride. She has been to Athens before but this is my first visit. And this is a first visit for both of us to Athena's."

"Oh!" Constantine exclaimed. "A new marriage! Congratulations. This is cause for celebration! May I make some recommendations?"

Constantine exuberantly flipped open the wine list and pointed to his personal favorite. I loved how full of life he was. Just like Fred.

"Retsina!" Constantine announced. "The Greeks have made this wine for thousands of years. It is a white wine with an unusual flavor because we age it in pine barrels. I think you will enjoy."

When he returned with our glasses, I tipped mine to my lips cautiously. With the first sip, the hint of the pine resin met my pallet—thus, the name, of course. I rolled the next sip around on my tongue, uncertain whether I liked it...but there was Fred, across the table, sipping his Retsina with utter freedom and joy, already discussing the specials and recommendations with Constantine.

"Tonight we are offering grilled lamp chops with garlic and lemon..." Constantine was saying.

How could I be my old hesitant self, in the presence of Life unbounded? *What the heck.* Once again, I opened myself to the adventure, lifted my wine glass and offered a silent toast: *To Life...bring it on.*

When our dinner arrived, five musicians in traditional Greek apparel had taken the stage playing quietly—one on a stringed instrument known as a bouzouki, and the others on a drum, wooden flute, violin and an eerie-sounding Greek clarinet. The instruments were not tuned to a traditional major scale, so the music was lively but it had a mystical quality.

We watched as the full moon rose over the Parthenon. I had decided on the swordfish and Fred chose the lamb chops. The meal was complemented with grape leaves, Greek yogurt, cucumber and garlic, bread and olives. We ate our dinners and sipped the Retsina ... and we drank in the mystery of life that had brought us all of this.

And then, the tenor of the evening shifted. Male dancers in traditional full-sleeved muslin blouses, black vests, and pleated skirts called a foustanella took to the dance floor.

The music started softly and slowly but increased in volume and tempo as the song played on; likewise the dancers started slowly with their arms linked over one another's shoulders as they formed a line. As the dance drew to its conclusion, the patrons were all standing and clapping in time with the downbeat of the music. People began shouting with the dancers as the pace of the dance rapidly increased. The dancers faced one another and the two men on either end linked their arms to form a circle.

When the circle was closed and the dancers' backs were to us, one of the patrons standing near us picked up a porcelain plate and threw it onto the floor where it smashed into a million pieces. And then another patron followed suit...and then another.

Seeing my delight and curiosity, Constantine stepped up beside me to explain.

"It is an ancient tradition. The throwing of plates has been given many meanings over the years. Some believe it is a way to cast out evil. Others that it as sign of abundance: we have so much more than we need that we can afford just to smash the plates as we have plenty more."

"And some others say," as he winked at Fred and I, "that the breaking of plates was a custom begun by parting lovers, so that each of the lovers would be given half of the plate...in case fate somehow separated them and so that they would be able to recognize one another again even if many years had passed."

Constantine paused to see if his audience was receptive. Seeing that Fred was hanging on his every word, he continued, "My personal favorite explanation is that when one experiences irrepressible joy, the Greeks call this Kefi, that the soul and the body are overwhelmed with exuberance and there must be an outlet. So the Greeks throw plates as an expression of irrepressible joy."

Constantine smiled and handed a plate first to me and then to Fred and we were caught up in the enthusiasm of the evening and we joined the others in the smashing of the plates as we cheered on the dancers.

Later that night at the inn Fred slept deeply but I was restless and awake. Was this just the time change and jet lag messing with my sleep? I lay still and tried not to wake him.

I thought about the exuberance and joys of the evening. Random thoughts filled my head as I waited for sleep to come. They would never allow the throwing of the plates in the States, someone could get hurt and lawsuits would ensue. I had seen the myriad of porcelain pieces that littered the floor around the dancers' feet...

And there was something else…the thought of lovers parted by fate.

Why would they need the pieces of a broken plate to recognize one another? If they were truly in love, would they not just know one another without regard for time or place? I concluded that they would. The thought of lovers parting, while I was lying beside my beloved, was just too sad to think about…

I pushed the notion from my mind and shifted my focus.

Stay present, count your blessings and I moved in closer to Fred….

All through this trip I had been nudged by thoughts of the spirit world and yet been cognizant of the joys of living in this one. These two worlds seem to be inextricably intertwined and woven together. And yet when the spirit breaks free, and I had seen this in Fred, as well as in the dancers tonight, there is a joy and an overwhelming exuberance for life and living. When I was in Fred's presence my spirit soared and I, too, got caught up in this irrepressible joy as I lived this moment and anticipated the life that was unfolding before me.

As I snuggled in close to Fred and as sleep began to invade my consciousness, I decided that I was in agreement with our server. The plates were thrown and smashed because the body and the soul are so overwhelmed with joy. This was something I could understand….

We traveled to Italy and spent time in Venice, Florence and Rome wining and dining, soaking in the culture and seeing the sites. Fred introduced me to total strangers as 'mia sposa' or my bride. People congratulated us, offered us drinks and toasted us with their best wishes.

More than one morning, as we left the inn, we were greeted by smiling patrons and innkeepers. Their smiles acknowledged that we were on our honeymoon.

Fred would return their smiles and laugh and I would blush and turn away as I am certain we made quite a racket in the middle of the night with the thin walls, the creaking bed springs and the sounds of unbridled passion as we made love on into the early morning hours. We had an insatiable desire for one another.

We traveled by train and took a self-guided walking tour of each city we visited. By the time we arrived in Sorrento on the Amalfi Coast, I had developed shin splints and my legs were aching in pain. Late one night as I sat in the chair in our hotel room, Fred washed and massaged my aching feet and wrapped my throbbing legs in warm moist towels.

Sometimes people tell you they love you and sometimes people show you. The words sometimes ring hollow, the acts of love never do. Fred loved me and I felt it in each and every tender caress.

As I allowed Fred to care for me I could not help but think of the Last Supper, as Jesus humbled himself to wash the feet of his disciples. It was a beautiful reminder that there are times in life when we are all called to serve.

We traveled to the Greek Islands. On the island of Santorini we had beautiful accommodations. We stayed in a small inn and our room had been carved into the lava rock. It had a private balcony with a spectacular view overlooking the bay and the volcano. It was the view one sees on post cards. We rented two mopeds and travelled all over the island. Our days would gently unfold.

The next stop was the island of Crete. We travelled by ferry from one island to the next. On the sea we had time to consult the guidebooks and discuss the options we had for the last few days of our honeymoon.

"I can't explain my fascination with ancient Greece. I probably should have been a history major." We snuggled close together on the lower level of the ferry, as the passage was cool and windy. "I really want to see the Palace of Knossos. I remember studying about the Minoan Civilization in high school and again in college." Fred held me close to him as he tried to keep me warm. He patiently listened as I rambled on. "This is certainly not my cultural heritage. If it were, that might explain my fascination, but I am Irish, Swedish and German." He nodded and acknowledged, as he was well aware of where I hailed from. I took another breath and continued, "There were classes that I elected to take in college and I had a distinct feeling that I knew the material before it had been taught. It was an eerie déjà vu sensation."

Fred just smiled at me. In the culture and religion I had grown up with, if I spoke of this I would be seen as a complete wacko. All my life I have kept this type of thing to myself. Fred was the first person that I felt safe enough to talk to about this and to my great relief he did not consider me a heretic.... or even your regular run of the mill nut job.

We decided that while we were in Crete we would take a trip to the Palace of Knossos as well as a hike 10 miles down the Samarian Gorge.

The next morning we lingered too long in our hotel room in the City of Iraklion.

"No mopeds. No scooters. They are all gone. You are too late." The proprietor of the bike shop stood on the sidewalk where a few motorcycles were parked. He looked at his watch and scowled as if to say, if you wanted mopeds you should have been here earlier.

He picked up on my disappointment as Fred and I tried to come up with a Plan B.

"Lady, look it is no problem. You take this little motorcycle and sit behind your husband. It will be good. You like it. You see." He was trying to be accommodating but he also had his own agenda and did not want to lose the day's rental.

I was hesitant. My work as an emergency room nurse had left me with graphic memories of victims of motorcycle accidents. Fred acknowledged my reluctance. But the reality was that it was nearly mid-day and if we didn't get on with it we would not see the palace today, and after last night's discussion on the ferry he knew that I did not want to miss it.

"It is your decision honey. Either way is okay with me." No pressure. He said it and he meant it. The decision was mine.

There was my hesitancy again.

"Okay. Let's do it. Please be careful." Reluctantly, I gave my consent, against my better judgment.

We rented the motorcycle. Fred drove and I rode behind him holding on to him for dear life. The palace was a short ride away and the day was sunny and warm. I wrapped my arms around Fred and I moved in close behind him as if we were two pieces of a puzzle.

48

I know that he would have liked to open the bike up and go for a real ride. Too bad for him that I am such a coward and was terrified. He honored my wishes and rode slowly and stayed off the busy roads as we meandered the back roads towards the palace.

The Palace of Knossos was built during the Bronze Age somewhere between 3000 and 1100 BCE by the Minoans. They built the palace on the wealth acquired by trading with other ancient civilizations as far away as Scandinavia.

We spent the afternoon walking about the remains of the ancient palace. I was mesmerized and Fred embraced the experience with equal enthusiasm.

We stayed until closing, and as we left, the guard locked the gate behind us. We walked arm in arm out to the parking lot. We were so engrossed in the visit to the palace that I had forgotten all about the motorcycle, if only temporarily. The lone motorcycle awaited us.

We both stood there looking at the bike. Fred opted for a diversionary tactic. "Are you hungry?" he ventured.

"I'm starving." I conceded, "Do you want to find a little café close to the hotel." I suggested. Thinking let's just get rid of this motorcycle. I did not want to go for a joy ride and Fred knew it, but we did have to get the bike returned. There was no way around that.

Fred climbed on the bike and started the engine. It started up easily. He looked over his right shoulder and gave me a look that said, "Get on the bike. It's time to go."

I straddled the bike and moved in close to him, carefully placing my feet on the foot holders. The monolog ran on in my head as we pulled out of the parking lot. I don't even know what they call these foot holders, certainly not stirrups. I remember feeling cold as our bodies cut through the late afternoon air. It was much more comfortable to ride during mid-day, but now the sun was moving towards the horizon and I was cold again. I am always cold. I was wishing for a sweater or a jacket, long pants, socks and shoes but instead I am wearing shorts and sandals. I moved in close behind Fred and I used his body to shield mine from the wind. I held on tightly as we made our way back to the city. I consciously tried to relax, to enjoy the moment and suspend the fear that loomed just behind the exhilaration of being on this flying machine.

We rode the motorcycle back towards the hotel in search of some local cuisine for dinner.

What happened next, has taken on a surreal quality and exists in my memory like a series of photographs.

Fred turns down a hill on a narrow side street.

I feel my body tip into Fred's as he angles the bike around the first curve.

The street is covered with loose gravel and road oil.

There are skid marks left in the road.

I press my body closer to Fred as he takes the next turn.

He seems to have the bike under control. I breathe.

As we take the next curve the back tire of the bike begins to slide on the loose gravel.

The bike is tipping to the right.

Fred shifts his weight and struggles to rebalance the bike.

In that instant I know that we have tipped too far.
 We begin to fall.

We are falling.

The motorcycle slides out from under us.

I try to protect my face as the road rushes at me.

I try to catch myself with my hand.

I am on the road.

The gravel digs into my hands, my forearms and my knees.

My skin is torn and stained with grit and oil from where I hit the road.

Fred is lying down the hill in the road.

He is not moving.

The bike is even further down the hill.

"Oh my God, Oh my God."

I hear my own voice as I repeat this over and over again.

I cannot stop myself. I am hysterical.

I am on my feet and Fred is already at my side.

"Are you okay?" He asks with urgency and concern.

His hands are bleeding and his arms are scraped. His shorts are dirty and torn.

I am hysterical and cannot focus.

My hands and knees are bleeding and embedded with gravel.

I am not hurt and neither is Fred.

Our wounds are superficial, only skin deep.

I am inconsolable.

I stand there and cry.

Fred wraps me in his arms.

"Are you okay?" he asks again.

"I'm okay, I'm okay, I'm okay." I hear the words coming from me. I repeat this over and over again. I try to let the words sink in.

I am shaken to the depth of my soul.
The terror seizes me.
I have had an epiphany.
Fred and I are okay but in this moment I see clearly.
Everything that I hold dear can be lost in an instant.

Fred pulls the bike from the middle of the road and parks it.
He calls a cab and takes me to the hotel.
I am no longer hungry.
I lie down on the bed and cry myself to sleep.

When I awoke it was night.
Fred has returned the bike, been to the pharmacy for antiseptic and bandages and brought us dinner to eat in the room.

We cleaned and bandaged one another's wounds. And again he told me, "I am so sorry."

I was calmer now and I tried to reassure him, "You do not need to apologize, it was an accident and we are both okay."

As I held him tight and we fell asleep in one another's arms, my last conscious thought was that I had totally overreacted to what was only a minor mishap. No matter how I tried to convince myself of this… the truth is that it did not feel like it. Neither then or now. But the rest was healing as we slept away the trauma of the day.

The next day we rose early and traveled to the Samarian Gorge for a daylong hike. The night's rest had helped me to shift gears emotionally and embrace this new day and the adventure it would bring. I met the day with gratitude for my good fortune; I consciously chose not to focus on what might have been.

I was amazed that someone who knew me so well could love me in my entirety. How did I get so lucky? My spirit opened and received the grace that had been bestowed upon me. I have a husband, a lover, and a friend who actually understands me. We are on a spiritual path. Everyday our lives became richer as I experienced the depth of his being and our lives became more and more intertwined. This was a miracle and it was not lost on me.

In the years to follow a friend would look at our lives and would come to understand our journey and in doing so he compared us to pair skaters. I think the analogy is a beautiful one. For pair skating involves a man and a woman whose performance gives the impression of two skating as one. Pair skating is beautiful and yet very difficult as it requires similar technique and timing as well as practice and trust between the partners and it is not without risk as serious accidents are common. A prophetic analogy indeed.

It had been a wonderful honeymoon but after three weeks it was time for us to return home. We flew from Athens to London on TWA Flight 847 and then on to JFK Airport in New York and home to Detroit Metro.

Two weeks later, Lebanese Shia extremists would hijack the same flight, TWA Flight 847. The passengers and the aircraft staff were held hostage for two weeks. One of the passengers was beaten and killed. I followed the story as it unfolded over the national news. In this enlightened moment it was all very clear to me ... life can change in an instant and I had so much to lose. Death had just missed us twice. It came for others but not for me. Not for us.

A few narrow misses and life goes on. I lost myself in my own thoughts. I pondered the near misses and the circumstances and chance events that kept us just this side of the spirit world.

Clearly the spirit world is just *a breath away.*

Is this what I was supposed to pay attention to? Is there something here that I needed to learn? Oh yes, there but for the Grace of God go I.

CHAPTER 4

Bliss

We returned home and enjoyed a bliss-filled summer as we settled into married life. I have heard many people say that the first year of marriage was the most difficult for them. It was not that way for us.

My office was about 35 miles from where we lived. On a good day it was a 55-minute commute and other days I caught rush hour traffic in both the City of Pontiac and the City of Detroit, and if there was a train or an accident my commute time would double and it frequently did. Fred worked 10 minutes from the house. So I would leave before he did in the morning and return after him at night. Most nights he had dinner prepared and the candles lit for a romantic dinner. Some nights he picked me up on the dock with the sailboat, and a picnic and a bottle of wine. Yes, I was blessed and my blessing had human form.

We spent the summer in the garden and on the lake. We entertained family and friends. I grew in appreciation of Fred; everyone thought he was their best friend and confidant. The reality was that he was my best friend and I was his. We willingly shared our lives with the people that we loved.

Fred's job was demanding. He was an assistant prosecutor in Oakland County. He worked in the Circuit Court division. This meant that he prosecuted those accused of the most heinous crimes: murder, rape and other forms of violence or capital crimes involving major theft. Fred was very good about separating his responsibilities at work with his personal life. Unless there was a funny quip or story, he usually left his work at the office. If the case he was working on was particularly gruesome or heinous, he did not want to talk about it at home. I had worked in the emergency room in Detroit. It is not that I was squeamish but I understood that he did not want to taint what was beautiful by focusing on what is foul and nasty. He needed a break from his work to keep balance in his life, and our home provided him a refuge.

There is much to be balanced in life in order to live successfully; the Greeks speak of finding the golden mean. As we learned in Crete, when there is gravel on the path, life can so quickly and easily slip out of balance. We consciously worked for balance and strove for that golden mean.

Fred and I spoke about having children. Fred was uncertain, his parents had a rocky marriage and he feared losing what we had. But he knew, before we married, that I wanted children and he wanted me to have the life I had always dreamed of. I think that is what real love is: caring about the happiness of another person.

My job and the extended commute were exhausting me. We discussed the pros and cons of my looking for a new job closer to home. I was almost 29 and Fred was 35.

One afternoon he called me at work, "I won my case. I'm ready, let's have a baby." We laughed and talked about trying to have a baby when we returned from our winter vacation in Costa Rica.

I was pregnant the first month we tried. We were elated and our bond deepened.

Two weeks into my pregnancy my brother's baby boy was born with a genetic condition affecting the long bones of his arms and legs. Fear crept in. Would the child I was carrying also be afflicted? We needed answers.

My obstetrician recommended genetic counseling. An ultrasound was ordered. Fred and I met with Dr. Lester Weiss to discuss the results of the ultrasound. Dr. Weiss was an old soul of infinite wisdom and he reassured us that our baby would not be afflicted with the same genetic issue that my nephew has, but he asked us to consider what it meant to be a parent. Were we willing to embrace the children that we would have in all of their humanity and with all of the uncertainty that life brings? We contemplated the vastness of this question as we thought about the unknown and the unknowable and the life that grew within me. The doctor did not seek an answer from us but rather posed the question and it hung before us.

On the way home in the car, Fred and I talked about the unknown and the unknowable. We concluded that to fully participate in the fullness of what life has to offer one must learn to trust. We decided that we were ready for wherever this journey would take us.

Late in my pregnancy I was shopping in town and as I walked past the glass windows I caught the reflection in the glass. Oh, no, that large woman could not possibly be me. But she was a redhead and she was wearing my coat. My word, when did I get to be so enormous? I checked out the reflection. My coat still buttoned. How big could I possibly be? I turned around to check out the reflection of my backside in the glass and to my horror the back pleat of my coat was wide open. So this was why the coat still buttoned. Life certainly has a way of teaching us what we need to learn, and this was another lesson in humility.

Mid-November I was at a routine doctor's appointment and my obstetrician told me I needed to go to the hospital because I was in labor. I didn't believe it because I had no pain. She assured me that some women go through labor without any real pain. I was delighted because I am the world's biggest coward when it comes to pain. I had feared labor and delivery from the day I learned where babies came from. I played with the notion that perhaps God knew this and was going to grant me a painless childbirth.

I told the doctor that I couldn't possibly go to the hospital. I wasn't ready. I was afraid. Afraid of the pain of childbirth and afraid that something might go wrong. I was afraid that I would die in childbirth and afraid that there might be a problem with the baby. There were too many variables and they were all beyond my control and I was afraid of being out of control.

I called Fred and he met me in the labor and delivery suite at the hospital. In my very human condition, like all other mothers, I was not to have a painless delivery. It was only false labor. After five hours of fetal monitoring they sent us home and I was still pregnant.

Two weeks later while we were putting up the Christmas tree, I reached up to hang an ornament on one of the upper branches and my water broke. I called my doctor and she told me to go to the hospital. I still didn't have any contractions, so we took our good sweet time. And we sat around in the labor room all afternoon and nothing happened. The doctor decided to send me to the post-partum unit, where the mothers who had already delivered their babies were. The plan was that tomorrow they would induce labor.

I did not want to go. I did not want to be induced. I had heard the horror stories; it hurts even more than regular labor. I am a coward when it comes to pain. The nurse consented to let me get up and walk to my room. I didn't get around the corner and the first contraction hit. I doubled over in pain. The nurse who was accompanying us was certain I was faking. I saw her roll her eyes; no doubt she thought I was a drama queen. We continued to walk to the room and by the time we got there I was in hard labor. Reluctantly, the nurse put me in the wheelchair and took me back to the labor room.

I would like to say that I was infinitely brave and strong but that would not be the case. I felt like a train wreck, completely out of control, but then our beautiful baby boy, Cullen, was born. Fred broke into song and sang Happy Birthday to Cullen.

I took one look at my healthy new baby and my heart opened with the kind of love that a parent feels for their child. It was like nothing I had ever experienced before. The kind of love that knows no bounds and would sacrifice everything to keep those they love safe and well.

Later I would think: maybe this was the lesson of childbirth. Pain breaks open the heart...otherwise we seem to go through life unconsciously, avoiding the difficult and seeking only comfort.

If Fred had any reservations about fatherhood, they vanished completely with the birth of our son. We were blessed to participate in the miracle of new life. This was not lost on us. We wallowed in the joy and wonder of this new creation. I was in love with my beloved husband and our beloved son.

I made the decision not to return to my job. I could not imagine working 60 hours a week, not including the commute time. How would I ever see my baby? We were used to being a two-income family, but we adjusted and learned to live on our new budget. We lived in the abundance of grace and love. Our needs were few and we found that we had plenty. Life was good and every day I was mindful and grateful for the blessings of my life.

The seasons gave way one to the next and our hearts continued to give way to our new son. The temporary pain of childbirth had long since receded to a memory, and I felt that my grip on life was firmer and stronger than ever.

In late July, 1987, we spent a long weekend with our friends, Dan and Linda at Linda's parents' cottage on Glen Lake in northern Michigan. They were similarly situated as their first-born son, Guy, is 6 weeks older than Cullen. Our entire weekend was structured around the needs of our baby boys; their needs to eat and sleep set the agenda and we were all okay with that.

It is a beautiful day, eighty-five degrees, sunny and not a cloud in the sky. The lake is like glass.

I have finished nursing Cullen. He is wearing only his diaper and his little body is hot and sticky in my arms. He is finally asleep as I lay him down for a nap in the guest room. The fan whirls and provides a bit of a breeze and some white noise. I say a silent prayer that both of the boys will sleep, so they will not be crabby later. I am hot and sticky as I tiptoe out of the house to rejoin the adults on the beach.

Fred is spending the afternoon patiently trying to teach Dan to windsurf, but there isn't much wind and Dan has not met with much success. Learning to windsurf is not easy as it requires one to stand and balance as if on a surfboard, pull a water laden sail out of the water, to understand and implement the principles of sailing, to say nothing of the need for consistent wind. Dan has been on and off the board dozens of times during the past two hours while Fred patiently coaches him from the water. Both Dan and Fred have had enough of the lesson. The afternoon is still and hot.

I join Linda on the lawn chairs as we watch our husbands, and we pick up some strand of conversation that we had begun earlier before the needs of our children had taken precedence. Suddenly there is a hint of a breeze and it feels good against my hot moist skin.

Fred calls to me, "The wind is up and I'm going to go for a quick sail. I'll be back to help with dinner."

"Have fun." I call back to him. As Fred heads out across the lake, I watch and think, this is how it is supposed to be done. He stands tall and strong as he holds the red and yellow sail. It is taut with the wind. His board is skipping over the tops of the white caps that appear on the far side of the lake. He is moving rapidly away from the shore line... just as a black tornado cloud complete with gale force winds and torrential rains comes over the Sleeping Bear Sand Dunes. Fred disappears from sight and the winds begin to blow the lawn chairs off the deck.

Linda and I gather up the towels and the beach paraphernalia that are strewn about the beach. The sand stings my legs and I turn my face away from the lake to keep the blowing sand from my eyes.

Linda and I close the windows to the cottage as the sand from the beach is being blown through the screens. The lights flicker and power goes out. No one comments. We all know that it will not be flickering back on any time soon.

I stand with Dan and Linda. We look out the picture window towards the lake. We watch for any sign of Fred. There is no sign of him.

The storm rages and I am paralyzed with fear.

"I'm going to look for Fred." Dan offers to take the ski boat out to see if he can find Fred. He is not asking for permission. I nod, although I know he is not looking for my approval. He kisses Linda and is out the door and Linda and I follow.

I am grateful. I know this decision puts Dan at risk as well. Linda and I cling to one another at the shoreline as Dan starts the boat. He turns the boat into the wind and makes several attempts to pull away from the shore but the wind and the waves repeatedly crash the boat into the shore. There is no way to launch the boat over the waves that crash angrily on the shoreline. We begin to see the full force of the storm. It is gut-wrenching to feel so impotent against the powers of nature.

"Where in the name of God is he?" I am frantic and fall down on my knees on the dock begging God for the safe return of my beloved. The sand is blowing and stings my exposed skin. The sky is black, and the rain blankets and obscures my vision. I can see nothing. The wind howls and cries of death and destruction. "Where, dear God, is Fred? Please, I beg of you, please bring him back to me. I need him. We need him. Please." Repeating this prayer aloud again and again, I look to God for mercy as the storm rages all around me.

The futility of my pleas is obvious to Linda; with clarity she sees that we are also in danger if we stay on the dock. Wordlessly, she pulls me to my feet and leads me toward the house, and I follow.

Dan docks and ties the ski boat and then decides to take the rowboat out to see if he can find Fred. Dan is not a small man. The force of the wind picks up the rowboat with Dan in it and turns the boat upside down on the dock completely covering Dan. We are all panic-stricken at this point.

"No more heroics, Fred would never stand for this. I cannot ask you to put yourself in this kind of danger." I know in my heart of heart it has to be this way. There is no verbal acknowledgement. We all fall silent and retreat to the house and watch for Fred from behind the plate glass window.

The temperature has dropped. We are cold and wet from the rain and the winds. I shiver and Linda offers me a blanket from the bed. The rowboat is blown off the dock and hits the electric light post, completely severing it at the ground level. There are ship-to-shore docking stations rolling end over end along the shoreline. Trees are being uprooted and falling all around the cottage. The sky is black and the rain falls in thick blankets, causing a complete visual obstruction. I am awestruck by the power of the storm. Where is my beloved? I beg and plead to God. I can see nothing. The minutes open up like horrible chasms. I fall silent as I wait in continual silent prayer. I stand and watch for any sign of Fred. There is nothing. It has been 40 minutes since I last saw him.

My mind will not be still. If the storm is this severe on the shore what is it like in the middle of the lake? Was he wearing his life vest? I don't think so. I ask and answer. I try to keep the panic away. I do not allow myself to consider the potential disaster. These thoughts creep in unbidden. How will I survive without him? Who will help me raise my child? Will Cullen never know his father? I push the thoughts away. The tears roll down my face. I keep watch.

"There he is!" Dan sees Fred. The sail is down and Fred is carrying his board. He is walking along the shoreline. Dan and I rush to meet him. I am crying and offering up prayers of gratitude to The Almighty as I run towards him.

Dan helps Fred hold onto the sail and the board that are being pushed about in the wind. "Get back in the house." Fred is stern as he sends me away. He speaks to me in an authoritative way that I am not accustomed to. Fred has never spoken to me this way before. I take him seriously and consent to wait inside, for he is thinking clearly and I am emotionally distraught. I understand that he is fearful that he will lose control of the board or the sail in all the wind, and a flying object or a falling tree will hurt me.

Once Fred and Dan have secured the windsurfer so that it could not become a projectile, he joined me in the cottage. The relief I felt knowing he was safe gave way to uncontrollable sobbing. Fred tried to assure us that he had been completely safe the entire time. All he did was lower the sail and lie on the board and ride the waves into the shore. We were not convinced.

He told us of an encounter with a father and a son in a ski boat who were also caught in the storm. They asked Fred if he wanted a ride to shore. "I thanked him but declined his offer. The father looked visibly relieved when I declined. I thought about it for a moment. What would I do with my board and sail? I was afraid that their boat might flip if I tried to get in while the waves were so rough." Fred continued to minimize the danger. He contended that we were probably in more danger on the land than he was on the lake. It did not feel like that to me. It felt like another near miss.

One of the babies began to cry and woke the other. The babies had slept through the entire incident. The storm had lowered the temperature considerably. Fred was chilled to the bone. There was no water for anything including a hot shower, as the electricity had knocked out the power for the well. We cuddled under the blankets as I attempted to warm him up and he to comfort me from my fears. He held me as I nursed our baby to soothe his crying. We were all back together. Despite Fred's reassurances, I was shaken and emotionally I felt I was on unsteady ground.

Later, we went into town for dinner. The level of destruction caused all the adults to go silent. There were large swaths of trees through the forest that were down. They looked as if they had been clear-cut by loggers. The power was out all over northern Michigan. The radio spoke of the wide-spread destruction. There was only one open restaurant in Glen Arbor, Art's Bar. They were grilling food on the sidewalk, as there wasn't any power. Everyone from the surrounding area was there milling about and swapping stories.

This lake front community is like any small town. These people know one another and have been looking out for one another for years. There was talk about the lone windsurfer. "Does anyone know who he is? Has anyone seen or heard what happened to him?" People all along the shoreline were watching and praying for Fred. When they met Fred this evening, the men shook his hand and the women hugged him and proclaimed it a miracle that he had survived. I think Fred began to realize the blessing that had been bestowed upon him and our family.

After dinner we drove out to the shore of Lake Michigan and walked along the beach. The storm had given way to a beautiful summer evening and the beginning of a beautiful sunset. There were dozens of large yachts that had been thrown ashore during the storm only to have the bottoms torn out of the vessels. We walked in silence as we witnessed the destruction.

What if I had lost him? Did God hear my prayer and the prayers of the others? Is Fred still here in response to an answered prayer?

"*According to an ancient plan not one of us gets out alive,*" the lyrics from a Greg Brown song rolls through my head.

Did God come for Fred today? How, in the name of God, could I go on if Fred had not survived? The questions haunted me. I had no answers, only questions. What if this was practice…another practice session…but practice for what?

Later that night as we lay awake in bed, Fred suggested "Perhaps it is time for us to address the spiritual needs of our family." I had been raised Catholic and Fred was raised Presbyterian. His family rarely went to church and when I was growing up we went every Sunday without fail. He told me that he thought it could be a good thing and less confusing for the children if we all went to the same church. "I am willing to consider Catholicism."

Cullen had been baptized in the Catholic Church when he was a few weeks old but I had never asked Fred to become Catholic. I believe there are many spiritual paths to God and people must find the path that is right for them.

I knew this would be hard for Fred. I had never really encountered any anti-Catholic sentiment until I met Fred's family. Now I understand that this anti-Catholic rhetoric reflected the prejudices commonly held by many Protestants. However, most people that I knew had the good sense and common courtesy not to speak these things aloud in my presence, as these remarks were clearly offensive.

From my perspective, Catholicism is one vehicle by which members of the human family find access to God. The Catholic Church has been revered in my family for generations, and for many good reasons, as the church has provided charity to the poor, health and medical care for the infirmed, and educated great numbers of people worldwide. In my mind's eye this is what Christ asked of his followers, that we care for one another.

In the years to follow, the sins committed by a minority of the Catholic clergy would come to light and the anger felt by the world would be mirrored by the Catholic faithful, myself included. But it is also unfair to judge the entire Church and the lives of service given by most of the clergy by the behavior of the minority, no matter how heinous and reprehensible.

Fred had been a religion major when he was in college. He used to joke that he studied religion because it did not require him to take any classes in math or science. The truth of the matter was that he found the study of religion and spirituality fascinating, but had a difficult time with any religion that proclaimed to have the only pathway to the Divine at the exclusion to all other pathways.

Although I had been raised Catholic, we held this belief in common. If Our Creator does indeed love us, and we both believe that to be true, how could Our Creator only allow people who were born into Christian homes to be destined for salvation, and all other souls to be destined for damnation? This defies my understanding of love. We both struggled with this. So instead of joining a religious community or a church, we had spent most of our time together living in our own idyllic existence. We had just postponed making any concrete decisions about joining a church. It had been easier not to, until today.

Still, I held to my Catholic faith. For generations the women in my family had been the keepers of the faith. My mother's family was Catholic and lived in Northern Ireland during the potato famine of the 1840s. They were persecuted for their religion and had to flee their homeland to keep from starvation while the food that they grew as field hands was being exported to England. My family held firm to their religion and it cost them. For the sake of my ancestors and the sacrifices they made, I could not be the one who dropped the faith. I feel a real sense of obligation to keep the faith as a way to honor those who have come before me.

In my father's family it was my maternal great-grandfather who was anti- Catholic. My grandmother told me stories of her father burning the hats to keep his wife and the children from attending Mass, as it was part of the social protocol of the time that women should cover their heads in a Catholic church. My great-grandmother was a strong woman and was not about to be told what she could or could not do, even by her husband. She pinned a handkerchief on her head and the heads of her daughters as she took her seven children to church. My foremothers sacrificed a great deal to assure that the faith was not lost. I understand what is expected of me. I do not take this responsibility lightly.

I am a traditional woman in many ways. My life experience has taught me to honor the diversity of others because I believe that everyone has something to contribute. This includes my spiritual heritage as my Irish-Celtic ancestors have a long-honored tradition of seeing the sacred, the holy and the spiritual in everyday life and living. I am not 100% certain what it was that my ancestors struggled so hard to protect, but perhaps it was their right to choose their spiritual path to the Divine and maintain their cultural identity. Either way, I will not be the one who loses the way. Being Catholic is part of my cultural and spiritual inheritance. But I do not think this is the only way and I would not impose this path on my husband. If he follows this path it would be of his own choosing.

Fred would struggle with his decision to become a Catholic and would need a great deal of reassurance, particularly at the beginning, that this was the right decision for him. I think I can speak for him when I say that he thought it was important for him to pick a path and work towards a closer walk with the Divine than to debate which path was the right one. Years later, Robert Hazard, my sister Susan's husband, would write a song where he says that *we can get there 10,000 ways, 10,000 ways.* I believe that to be true and so did Fred.

As summer ended we began to make plans to return to church. The incident at the lake made us realize that *we know neither the hour nor the time* (Matthew 23:36) when we will be called to transition from this life to another. It was time to make certain we were not left unprepared. We discussed our options and in the fall of 1987, Fred began the RCIA program- Rite of Christian Initiation. After completing eight months of instruction, he would decide to join the Catholic Church. It was a difficult decision for him and he struggled with it.

Denis Naeger, a former Catholic Brother and Director of Family Life Ministry, ran the program at our local parish with the Pastor Father William Murphy. They eased many of the difficulties for Fred because they were people who lived and loved easily. They encouraged Fred's intellectual and spiritual questioning. They loved Fred and he them. He would cherish their friendship in the years that followed. But in the end, like most spiritual journeys, there comes a time when one must make a leap of faith and Fred took the leap.

Along this journey, Fred and I encountered folks who bought into the catechism of the church without question or concern, but we also encountered others who were much less rigid in their interpretation. He found a place of comfort knowing that the Catholic Church is made up of a wide variety of people and that Catholics are not simply clones who are told what to believe and how to behave, but there are also free thinking people amongst the clergy and the parishioners. Fred studied the Catholic mystics who seek union with the Divine and he began to see that there may be a place for him and his individual faith journey. I have known this part of my Catholic heritage all my life, but I fear the ultra conservatives within the church color outsiders' perceptions when they demand conformity of opinion rather than an open search for the miraculous, and encounters with the Divine.

We developed some new friends through our association with the church. These friendships would enrich our lives immeasurably. It helps to associate with people who have actively cultivated an awareness that they are on a spiritual journey. Our lives would become intimately intertwined with these folks: Colleen and Frank Zematis and Jill and Denis Naeger. We all had young children at the time and this gave us some commonality, but our friendships were anchored in something more. We would call on each other in the years to come, as the winds of change would shake our worlds. We would be given the opportunity to be Christ to one another; to bear one another's burdens and share one another's joys.

But this was a time of palpable joy as Fred joined the Church during the Easter Vigil service. Denis Naeger sang the ancient hymns acapella in a way that stirred the soul and illuminated the spiritual path that Fred and I were on.

We began spending more and more time with my parents. They loved spending time with their grandson, Cullen. Mom was always there to lend a hand and to assist with whatever needed to be done. She is clearly the unsung hero in this story as she lives to be of use and of service to others. Fred and Dad got close. They played tennis, went sailing, and generally enjoyed being in one another's presence. Fred would call Dad when he needed advice on something. When we were considering a major purchase, investment advice and sometimes just to chat. Dad joked that Fred always asked his opinion and then did whatever he wanted anyway, but the truth is Dad liked to be consulted and Fred benefited from his wisdom. Dad and Fred developed a father-son bond that Fred did not have with his own father. They grew in love and mutual respect.

The same week that I learned that I was pregnant with our second child, Grandma began to experience confusion. I took her to an internist who thought she might have had a stroke. I didn't think so. I called my friend, Lynne, whose husband is a neurosurgeon. I had an appointment for Gram the next day. They did a CAT scan and determined that she had a brain tumor. Our family was devastated. How could we break the news to her? The neurosurgeon, Harold, thought the tumor was inoperable and growing rapidly. He recommended a course of steroids to decrease any increase in intracranial pressure. His prognosis was 6 months to a year.

To focus on her dying diminishes the strength of her life and the role this woman had in my life. She lived simply and honorably with joy and gratitude for the life she was given. The tumor grew quickly and she deteriorated rapidly, and during the last few weeks of her life she was moved to an extended care facility.

The last time I visited her was in the extended care facility. Gram had been there for only a couple of weeks. The decision to move her had been difficult but necessary as she had deteriorated rapidly and needed full time care. It was in early March. Fred had come home from work and was caring for Cullen so that I could go and visit Gram. Last week when I was there she had slept most of the time, and when she was awake she was restless and agitated.

The daylight was waning as dusk settled in and I entered the facility. How had it come to this? Would this be where Gram would spend her last days? I had a very hard time with this. Mom and Dad both worked but I am a registered nurse; I should be caring for her. But I was pregnant and had a rambunctious two-year old. We had been around and around the issue and no one liked the reality of the situation, which was that Gram was dying, and she could need 24 hour care for months.

This place isn't too bad as far as nursing homes go. The florescent lights beam brightly overhead as I walk down the wide hallways with their linoleum floors. The hallways are tidy and smell faintly of disinfectant. At least it doesn't smell like urine. A nursing home; it does not seem like home in any way, shape or form.

An older woman in a wheel chair has dropped her lap robe. She is tied into the chair and struggles to recover the pink blanket. It has been hand-crocheted and laundered many times. I pick it up and cover her legs. She takes my hand and squeezes it gently. She cannot speak. It is so tough to grow old and lose independence.

I stop and check in at the nurses' station. It is always a good idea to be friendly with the nurses. A little sweetness goes a long way. These people work hard and I try to acknowledge this and express my gratitude. They need to know that someone cares for Gram and is checking in on her. She will get better care if they know that Gram is loved and lovable. People give a little more time and attention when their hearts are engaged in their work.

Gram is sitting up in bed, supported by a pillow, when I enter her room. Her hair has been combed, she is wearing her glasses and her nightgown is clean. She turns to look at me. "Hi Gram." I move towards the bed and give her a kiss on the cheek.

"Jeanne Marie. How is my girl?" I am 31 years old but I am still her girl. She smiles and I know she is happy to see me.

I pull a chair up close to the bed and we hold hands. "How are you feeling today?" I can tell that she is having a good day. It shows in her face.

"Your Dad was here this afternoon and that always makes my day and now you are here too."

We make small talk about what she had for dinner, how she is sleeping and whether she got up in the chair today? She voices no complaints but speaks kindly of the nurse's aid who assists her today. She is so much better than I have seen her in weeks. She is clear thinking today. She asks about Fred and Cullen and if I have heard from my sister, Susan. She calls her Suey Babe, just like when we were children. I linger at her bedside and we chat for 20 to 30 minutes when Gram's eyes wander off and she starts looking at the corner of the room near the ceiling. I follow her gaze. She appears to be listening and then she starts to laugh.

"Blanche, how long have you been here?" She waits as she listens for a reply. She laughs. "You've never met my granddaughter? My Jeanne Marie, Richard's daughter." She is in the midst of a conversation with someone that I cannot see. She is not afraid. Whoever is talking to Gram is clearly an old friend. I turn my head to the corner of the room and I cannot see anyone. I wait while Gram acknowledges something that is said to her and then she turns her face towards me.

"Jeanne, I want you to meet Blanche," and she looks me in the eyes and smiles a smile of great joy. She turns her head back to the corner of the room and is talking and laughing with someone that I cannot see.

Blanche is my grandmother's aunt, her mother's youngest sister. Blanche was a few years older than my grandmother and she has been deceased for many years before I was born. I know how much my grandmother loves Blanche, as over the years she has told me stories of the escapades from their younger days.

One moment Gram is smiling and talking to me, introducing me to Blanche, and the next moment she is laughing and joking with Blanche. Gram is not afraid. She is filled with joy.

The moment passes when the voice over the public address system announces, "It is now 8:00 and visiting hours are over."

I was upset by the experience but clearly Gram was not. She lay her head back on the pillow. She looked content. It was time for me to go. The tears rolled down my face as I kissed her on the cheek. "I love you Gram."

She smiled up at me, "I love you, too."

I cried all the way home in the car as I tried to wrap my head around what had just happened. In my mind the questions emerge and linger: When our time on earth is over, do those who have gone before come

76

to help us pass over? Are there times when the veil between the physical world and the spiritual world is so thin that we get glimpses of the other side? I was witnessing the destruction of the physical body of someone I greatly loved. But where does the soul go? We call it heaven but is heaven a physical place? Does the spirit need a physical place? My head could not make sense of it but my heart and soul understood. There is nothing to fear.

Four days later Gram passed. I grieved her passing as a part of me went with her the day God called her home. She was a remarkable person but she was also my guide. Little did I know how much I would need to heed her teachings in the years to come.

I was uncertain at the time what I had witnessed but it is now abundantly clear to me that Blanche's spirit was with us in the room. She had come to help Gram cross over. Gram was not afraid. I had witnessed the veil between two worlds. I know that there is so much more going on in the spirit world that we do not see.

Was there a reason why Blanche came to Gram while I was there... Was it to help me understand and not to be afraid? Later I would see the blessing.

Five months after Gram's passing, I was holding our second child. She is beautiful and pink and the sweetest little girl. We had discussed a few names but in the delivery room we made our final selection. She is to be named Gillian with a G, and she is my heart's delight.

Fred brought Gillian and I home from the hospital. It was a bright and beautiful sunny August day. When I walked in the house every room was filled with flowers. There were multiple bouquets of pastel-colored larkspur in every room. They were as beautiful and delicate as our beautiful baby girl.

Cullen was so happy to have his mom and his baby home. Life is good.

We adjusted to the newest member of our family. Fred took some time off work and spent time with all of us. He would take Cullen along on his daily adventures so I could rest and sleep when Gillian was sleeping, for we both seemed to be up all night, every night nursing.

At other times in my life I remember waiting for my life to begin...when I am done with college, when I find mastery in my work, when I am done with graduate school, when I find my career path...then my life will begin. My life is now. I savored every moment of the bliss I felt by sharing my days with someone who loved me for the person I am, complete with my faults, failings and very human frailties; he saw me in the best possible light and loved me. This is rare indeed. I had a deep sense of gratitude for the blessings in my life, for my husband, and for my healthy and beautiful son and daughter. I was indeed blessed and I knew this.

We loved our home on Elizabeth Lake but it was really better suited for a couple than it was for a family. We talked to a few contractors about renovating the house but the project was overwhelming. The renovations would cost more than the house was worth. In the end we decided to move.

The new house had been on the market for over two years. At the time, that was considered excessive. The house had a few problems. Okay, it had more than a few problems. The first time Fred saw it he referred to it as a "barking dog" . . . but I saw it differently. The house was in a small community of historic homes on a dead end street. The landscaping was so overgrown that it was difficult to see the house from the road. Perhaps this was a good thing as the exterior was atrocious. The house was built in the 1920s and had been added onto repeatedly without the benefit of an architect. The siding was painted gold on the front of the house and was installed horizontally, and the siding on the addition was white and had been installed vertically. Nice. What were these people thinking? The original classic wooden columns holding up the front porch had been replaced with black wrought iron curlicues. Clearly the exterior was an abomination in this neighborhood of historically authentic homes. Why did we even go inside? Location, location, location. The house was located on a small lake one block from the village. There was a no motorboat ordinance and the lake was spring fed, deep, and the water was clean. The house sat on a double lot and had 200 feet on the water of this pristine lake.

The inside was also a bit of a problem as there were three kitchens and one of them did not have a sink. The only internal entrance to the master bedroom was through the only first floor bathroom. There were three doors in the master bedroom that led outside. And there was wallpaper on everything.

Fred joked, "They wallpapered everything except the toilet seats."

This was not too far from the truth and most of the wallpaper featured poultry of some variety. Yikes!

I thought these oh so very minor flaws could be remedied. I wanted to live here. Fred began to see the vision of what was possible. He invited his sister to come look at the house before we decided to make an offer. We turned around and Shelley had disappeared without weighing in one way or another. Her absence spoke volumes. We decided to buy the house anyway. Only later did Fred admit to me that when we were at the closing, that he felt like vomiting.

We moved in on St. Patrick's Day. Cullen was three and Gillian was 5 months old. It was a throwback to another time as the neighbors stopped by to welcome us with gifts of homemade soup or cookies. We met more people in the first week in our new home than we did in the five years in our last neighborhood. This would be a good place for us to call home.

Our new home provided us with a bedroom suite on the first floor and the children's bedrooms were upstairs. The configuration was perfect for providing Fred and I with some private space of our own. At the end of a long day with the kids, housework and renovations, I was happy to climb into bed with this handsome man. We were almost always in bed by ten o'clock. Our bodies needed rest and release from the demands and tensions of the day. Most nights we would get into bed naked, just in case. I love to sleep naked and feel the cool sheets against my skin on warm summer nights and the heat of Fred's body when the winter winds blew. As I settled in after the rush of the day was over, Fred would often reach over and take one of my feet in his hands and begin to massage it and I would coo with gratitude as my dogs were always aching. He was ready, willing and able and I did not turn him down. His hands would slowly move up my legs and he would massage my calves and then my thighs and when I could not hold on a moment longer, I would turn to hold him as he would slowly and gently kiss and caress the most intimate parts of my body, until I was more than ready for him. Soon we were intertwined and intimately connected in a passion that would not let us rest. He filled me and fulfilled me and we were one. A sacred union. Two pieces of the whole.

My daily life demanded my full attention. I do not invent problems for myself. We lived in the moment and dealt with life as it presented itself. The love we felt for one another and our family was the balm for the little irritations of daily life.

And so in the summer evenings, we would walk into the village and down to the park at sunset. The sun would sink low and the sky was beautiful in hues of gold, blues and pinks. I would look at my family and our life and think about the beauty of our lives complete with color, texture and nuance. It was picture perfect.

We were not holy rollers. Our life was real and filled with little mishaps just like everyone else's. We joked, we teased, and we peppered our daily life with sexual innuendo, dirty jokes and occasional profanity. We are real and we made the best possible efforts to see the blessings of the day, and when given an option, we tried to see the people in our lives in their best possible light.

I remember thinking, "Life is good and we are blessed."

In the fall Cullen started preschool. He brought home every little virus, like little children do.

Over the course of the year every time one of the kids got a cold it progressed to pneumonia in Fred. The doctor kept prescribing antibiotics and didn't really think that much about it. It was strange for Fred to be ill, as he had always been the picture of health. Fred was a strong, healthy 40-year-old man. He exercised regularly, ate well, did not drink excessively and did not smoke. He was the poster boy for healthy living.

In the interim we had begun tearing the house apart. The wallpaper was the first to go. We stripped away the wallpaper one room at a time to find broken and cracked plaster in need of repair. All the walls were repaired and painted white, a blank canvas for the creation of our own home. The old carpet was torn up and discarded. We had beautiful hard wood floors underneath. We removed two of the three kitchens and completely renovated the original kitchen. I worked on the house during the day while the children napped but most of the work was a joint effort between Fred and I in the evenings.

I pushed forward. I wanted to get the house back together as Gillian was beginning to crawl and before long she would be up and running at full speed. Fred's energy level was dropping. We planned to tile the bathroom floors and I would find him napping with the kids. What had happened to my energetic partner? Fred would get us started on a project and Mom and I would finish alone. Fred was exhausted and I was getting irritated.

I had a passing thought that perhaps something may be wrong. A cloud passed quickly over the sun. I paused but did not get too concerned. All Fred's symptoms had reasonable explanations. He works hard, we have two small children, he is exhausted and I am too. I backed off on the renovation schedule. When well-rested, Fred was his cheerful good-natured self. I let it go.

There was no real reason for me to believe that life would bring me anything but joy. I had lost Gram, but even in her passing I had a sense of peace and a wonderful kind of lightness; for some reason I had been allowed to look, momentarily, through the veil to the spiritual world. I did not know that an event was coming, much like the dark storm cloud that threatened us on Glen Lake, but this time it would be a direct hit. Our journey deeper into love and thus into the Divine Presence of God would be the strength and foundation that we would cling to in the days ahead.

In the evenings when it was quiet and everyone else had fallen asleep, I would take a moment for myself and review the blessing of my life. I reflected on the beautiful spring day that Fred and I were married. It is hard to believe that it was over five years ago. How our lives had changed and grown in fullness.

For better or worse
For richer or poorer
In sickness and in health
To love and to cherish
From this day forward

Marriage vows are like two sides of the same coin. And it is a coin flip. One can be going along and everything is coming up roses and then the coin flips and life changes. This is what marriage is all about. In fact it is what life is all about. It is a journey and like any day's travel much is unknown and unknowable. Some days are wild and wonderful and totally unexpected but other days are frightening. Every life has the potential for great happiness and joy but also the potential for great tragedy and loss. It can all change with the flip of the coin. When the darkness comes and no one is watching this is when you find out what you are made of.

As for me I want *to keep to the sunny side, always on the sunny side, keeping to the sunny side of life* (Ada Blenkhorn). I want the good stuff; bring it on, I'm ready and waiting. Without being fully conscious of it, the truth is my life was so wonderful that I had begun to believe that God indeed favored me, and I had come to believe that this good life was somehow due me and my family and that by being good we had earned it. I don't know where these expectations came from but they had crept in, unbidden and had become woven into the fabric of my life.

CHAPTER 5

The Diagnosis

"Did you sleep okay? You were coughing all night." I asked in the morning as Fred put the kettle on for tea.

"Did I keep you up?" He answered with a question as he put the tea bag in the pot.

"No, but I can't believe that you slept very much. Maybe you should stay home today." I suggested as I started to fix Cullen's breakfast.

"Not today. I've got a pre-trial discovery on that murder trial and tennis tonight. You know I can't miss tennis." He smiled a reassuring smile and he gave me a pat on the ass as he left the kitchen with his cup of tea.

"I guess you must be feeling better." I called after him and he laughed. He never complained and always minimized his discomfort so I let it go. Again.

That evening the children had been fed, bathed, their teeth brushed, stories read, hugs and kisses goodnight had been given and lullabies sung until at last my two little angels were sleeping peacefully. I am uncertain who loved the bedtime routines more: them or me? I made my way downstairs to read for a little while and to wait for Fred.

Wednesday night he had his weekly tennis match. He was a tennis pro and gave lessons before he went to law school. This was Fred's idea of a night out with the boys. I wrapped the blankets around my legs as I settled in on the couch. The fire crackled softly and bathed the room in firelight. I opened my book and tried to determine where I'd left off. I delighted in these moments of quiet, as they were so infrequent. Before long I had lost myself in the story.

"Hey Honey." The door from the garage opened and Fred walked in. He set down his tennis bag and put his coat on the hook. He approached me as I sat on the couch and leaned over to kiss me.

I moved over to make a space for him next to me. "How was your game?" I replaced the bookmark and set the book aside.

"I played awful. I couldn't get to the ball tonight or return anything. Good thing Chris carried me." He was down and sounded dejected. "I might quit. Chris doesn't need an old man for a partner. He takes his game seriously and if I continue to play like I did tonight, he will be looking for my replacement."

I listened. "Maybe you just need to wait until you feel better. You are still on antibiotics from that last bout of pneumonia."

"Maybe, but that was not the problem tonight. The real issue is that my low back is killing me. I'm going to

86

shower, maybe the hot water will help." He struggled to get up off the couch. He placed his hands on his thighs and braced himself as he rose to standing.

"Can I fix you something to eat? I saved you some pasta and a salad." I asked as Fred headed toward the bathroom. He was leaning forward and walking slowly.

"That would be great. Can you get me some Advil, too?"

I walked into the kitchen to warm up the dinner and get the Advil. I could hear the sound of the shower as I worked about the kitchen.

Fred had slipped on the ice carrying an antique chair into the house about a month ago. He saved the chair but he wrenched his back. Backs can be tricky and they can take a long time to heal.

The next Tuesday, February 26, 1991, Fred was the lead prosecutor in a highly publicized murder trial. The jury selection was completed and Fred was supposed to deliver the opening arguments. He had been preoccupied with the case all weekend. Thoughts of Fred crept in as I set about my daily routine of housework and tending to the needs of the kids…I wondered how the trial was going.

The sound of the children's voices could be heard from the playroom and I was standing in the kitchen cleaning up after lunch when I heard the garage door go up. I dried my hands on a kitchen towel and carried it into the family room as Fred entered the house. He held his navy suit coat over his arm and the front of his white shirt was stained with bright red blood.

"What happened?" I tried to keep the panic out of my voice.

"I had another nosebleed. It started during my opening argument. Judge Anderson delayed the trial but I couldn't get the bleeding to stop. It lasted for over two hours. He had to adjourn the trial and send the jury home. I couldn't exactly address the jury with tissue stuffed up my nose and a bloody shirt." His frustration filled the room.

I followed Fred into the bedroom to help him out of his shirt. "Honey, you're burning up."

"I know. I feel like shit." He sat on the bed and removed his shoes and socks as I put the shirt to soak in the bathroom sink. I went into the bathroom to look for the thermometer. It was right in the bathroom closet where I had put it. Just two weeks ago Fred had pneumonia and had run a fever. I handed him the thermometer. He knew the drill, under the tongue for a full five minutes and no talking. He took off his dress pants and sat on the bed in his boxers. I took his clothes and hung them up and when I turned around he was under the covers, his eyes were closed and the thermometer was still between his lips. I checked the clock. Four and a half minutes. Close enough. I took the thermometer from his mouth and he opened his eyes to look at me. I turned the thermometer between my fingers so that I could read the mercury.

"103 degrees."

My mind raced, what the hell is going on? Infants and small children get fevers this high but not adults, unless they are dreadfully ill. This is another bacterial infection.

Fred had frequent nosebleeds. Initially his doctor thought it was due to respiratory irritation from all the renovations. He suggested we get a humidifier on the furnace and we did. But the nosebleeds continued. Next, Fred saw a specialist, an ear, nose and throat doctor. He found a small polyp in one of Fred's nostrils. He removed it in the office and cauterized the blood vessel. Problem solved, or so we thought, but now this.

Fred closed his eyes and pulled the covers up and around him.

"Honey, you need to take something for the fever." I placed the palm of my hand across his forehead and took a good long look at him as he lay there. He was gently shaking underneath the blankets.

"Okay, I'm freezing." He closed his eyes as I left the room to retrieve the Advil and a glass of water.

When I returned he took the tablets and only enough water to wash them down. I set the glass on a coaster on the bedside stand. "Honey, you need to go to the doctor." I started gently.

"I'm so tired, can't I just sleep for a while?" He asked, already well aware of what my answer would be.

"You are supposed to be in trial tomorrow." I played my ace in the hole in an effort to convince him to do what needed to be done. "You have some kind of bacterial infection and you need antibiotics. The sooner you start them the sooner you will be feeling better."

He sighed audibly. "Okay, let me see if I can get an appointment with Dr. Roberts." He rolled over and grabbed the portable phone off the nightstand and dialed the number. He knew the office number by heart. He asked to speak with one of the nurses. He described his symptoms and was told that there were no openings and he should go to the emergency room if he felt he needed to see a doctor.

He thought he was off the hook. He asked and they answered. He flopped back on the bed. Just making the phone call had exhausted him. I know that all he wanted to do was to sleep but I pushed on. "Honey, you need to go to the emergency room. I'll take you. Let me see if I can get a sitter."

"Okay." He covered up with the blankets and closed his eyes.

That was easier than I thought it would be. He must have been feeling awful, as he did not put up a fight. He just agreed. I went into the kitchen to call a sitter and no one was available.

I let him sleep for about an hour before I went to wake him. The Advil had kicked in and his fever was down. "Are you feeling any better?"

"A little."

"I can't get a sitter." Mom and Dad were in Florida and I couldn't reach Yvonne. My daytime options were limited.

"Do you think I need to go?" I know he wanted me to tell him no, that he could wait.

"I do." I sat on the bed beside him.

"Not the response I was looking for." He gave me a half-hearted smile and held my gaze.

"I know. Do you think you can drive yourself?" There is much that can be left unspoken when two people understand one another's hearts. So instead we focused on the practical issues of getting Fred to the hospital.

"Oh, yeah. Not a problem. Let me take a shower first. I'm all sweaty." He swung his legs over the side of the bed and sat there momentarily while he attempted to regain his equilibrium before he proceeded to the shower.

As Fred showered, I grabbed a note card and started writing a list of symptoms that Fred had been plagued with for the last 6 months. I wanted to be certain that all these issues were addressed: fevers, pneumonia, exhaustion, bloody noses, back pain and stiffness. As I composed the list I had a sense of impending doom. My anxiety grew. What if these were not isolated issues? Perhaps these disparate symptoms were somehow related. Could this be something systemic? I consciously pushed this gnawing concern from my head.

I handed Fred the list, as he got ready to leave. "Make certain you talk with the doctor about all of these. Please."

He looked over the list. "Okay." I gave him a hug and held on tight. We held one another by the back door. I wanted to go with him but I had no one to leave the children with. He knew this. Nothing needed to be said. It was understood.

"Call me when you know something." I whispered to him before I let him go.

"Will do. Love you." He grabbed the keys.

"I love you, too." I stood and watched as the door closed behind him.

Cullen and Gillian played with their toys in the family room as I prepared dinner. I watched the clock as the hours slowly ticked by and still no news from Fred. I fed the kids and cleaned up the kitchen. The phone rang. My girlfriend, Pamela Duke had called to chat. I explained that Fred had gone to the ER with a high fever and I was waiting to hear from him. I cut the call short and promised to call her soon.

I took the kids upstairs for their baths and the usual bedtime routine. It served as a good distraction for me. The kids chose their stories, and as I read aloud I kept the portable phone with me. When will I hear something? As I snuggled the kids into bed, we ran through the usual litany of prayers for all the people we love, and we also prayed for Daddy that he would be feeling better soon. The lullabies followed as I sang my children to sleep; before too long they were silently sleeping and I made my way back down stairs.

I tried to read my book but I was too distracted. I switched on the television, something I rarely did. There was a good reason for this as there was nothing on that I was interested in watching. I turned it off and headed down to the basement to switch the laundry. The clothes were warm from the dryer. They were soft and clean. I like to fold clean laundry. I sorted it into piles. I made a pile for each of us and then I created stacks of like articles: pants, t-shirts, underwear and lastly, I matched the socks. Laundry is one of the tasks of homemaking that I actually like. It goes in dirty and comes out clean and fresh, I fold it and back into its rightful place in the dresser drawer it goes. I can't believe I am thinking about this. I am a total head case. God damn it. When am I going to hear something? What is going on? Where is he? I put the laundry into two baskets. One basket was filled with the kid's stuff and one basket would go into our bedroom. Now what? I picked up the paper and re-read articles I read earlier in the day as well as the articles that did not interest me the first time through. They were still uninteresting.

I wait.

It was nearly ten o'clock when the phone rang. I caught it on the first ring.

"Hello."

"Honey. . ." It was Fred. He paused and then continued. "They are going to admit me to the hospital."

"What? What is the diagnosis?" I quickly transitioned into nurse mode.

He evaded the question and instead answered something else. "They initially thought I just had a relapse of pneumonia and were going to send me home with a prescription, but I told the doc that you would kill me if I didn't get these issues addressed. When I showed them the list, they reluctantly agreed to do a blood test."

"And," I proceeded gently now trying to keep the fear out of my voice.

He was gentle, treating me with the utmost care. He tried to protect me.

I asked again gently, trying not to alarm him. "What did they find?"

"My hemoglobin is 7 and I am in kidney failure." His tone was gentle as he stated the facts that I had pushed to hear.

"No! It cannot be! I'll call Shelley to watch the kids. I'm on my way." I could hardly think straight. All I knew was that I needed to be with him.

"Honey, it's late." He was resistant. "Besides they want me to go by ambulance downtown."

93

Not without me. It would take at least twenty minutes to make the arrangements and I could be there in forty. My brain was spinning. "If you have to go, by all means go, but I am on my way."

I called Fred's sister Shelley. She was up late watching TV with her husband Joel. I could hardly get the words out. Shelley knew this was not the time for a lengthy conversation. They too were on their way. I do not know how I got to the hospital. It is all a blur.

The doctors had no idea what was wrong but they needed to find out. My dear sweet Freddy was so ill. I could hardly bear to leave him at the hospital but he was so tired. His skin looked grey and pale under the florescent lights. They got him to his room and the nurse arrived to start an IV, put him on oxygen and get him into bed. It was well after midnight but there was still no rest for him, as the medical resident began the history and physical examination that were obligatory for admission. The tests were ordered. I sat and listened. Although it seemed like another lifetime ago, I had worked for years in the emergency room as a nurse. I understand the medical jargon and the implications of the tests that they were ordering. I was frightened.

When I left the hospital it was nearly dawn. The hospital was a 90 minute drive from home. I had plenty of time to think as I drove home. I went over the events of the day, the symptoms, the conversations with the doctor, the list of tests they were ordering and the fears I had for my beloved. When I would get to the end of the list I started again. I ruminated and was unable to break the circuitous thinking. My mind raced and I tried to quiet it with prayer. I begged God for help.

I don't know what's wrong. I don't like the sound of it. Please, Dear God, you have blessed me with a wonderful life. I am happy beyond my wildest dreams and expectations. When the children were born I experienced indescribable fear and pain but out of that pain I bore the magnificent blessings of my children. But for heaven's sake, Fred and I are on the right page. We don't need these lessons or a mid-course correction. Please, oh please, oh please, God, I beg you do not let this unfold into a tragedy for Freddy. For me. For our children. I beg you. Just fix it. He is the best man I have ever known and you know this too. How can you allow him to suffer so? He has never hurt anyone in his entire life. He loves you and he loves his life. He is kind and just and you know this better than anyone. Please let him rest well tonight and make him well. Just what is it that you want from me? Just name it and I will do it. Just make him well.

I begged and pleaded and then ranted and raved at God all the way home in the car. I vacillated from being the obedient child of God the Father, and then attempted to strike a deal with The Almighty who I know needs nothing from me, followed by wrath and fury and anger, and then I would start all over again. I was tortured with fear and worry. The reality was that I was most angry with myself. How could Fred have gotten this sick right under my nose, on my watch? What kind of a nurse was I? More importantly, what kind of a wife and partner was I?

Shelley and Joel were sleeping when I arrived home. I fell into bed with utter exhaustion and woke early when the kids climbed into bed with me. They were hungry and it was time for breakfast. Shelley and Joel woke to the everyday commotion of a household with little children and soon joined us in the kitchen for breakfast. They wanted to know what was going on with Fred; the questions could be read in their faces but they did not ask around the kids. So I fixed pancakes and we acted as if we had breakfast together every morning. Before too long the kids had finished and were off playing.

My explanation, to Shelley and Joel, was inadequate. I just did not know. I tried to keep to the facts that I did know and that was simply that they were planning to do more testing. Shelley changed her plans and did not go to work so she could stay with the kids. This allowed me to go back to the hospital to be with Fred.

"Thank you." My eyes filled with tears as I went to the bedroom to make some arrangements. I was on autopilot. My memories of this morning are sketchy at best. I must have called Ron, Fred's boss, as Fred was supposed to be in court. I am certain I called Yvonne, my faithful sitter, as she took care of the children the remainder of the week, but I have lost the details. My preoccupation with worry about Fred had numbed my senses. I called my parents in Florida and they made plans to return home. I could not be in two places at once; both Fred and my children needed me and I needed help.

These thoughts evaded my consciousness at the time. I was far too overwhelmed just dealing with the events of the moment. Upon reflection, I see so clearly how life can change in the blink of an eye. These changes can catch you unaware and unprepared. One moment I was firmly entrenched in my happy life, and then...

Over the next few days Fred was put though a myriad of tests. I waited with him. He continued to run a fever. The chest x-ray revealed pneumonia, again, and they loaded him up with even stronger IV antibiotics. There was a continual parade of doctors and they all asked the same questions and ordered more tests. No one had any answers, only more questions. I speak their language. I did not like the sound of this. A hospital is a terrible place to try to get well as no one ever sleeps including the patients.

Fred was so thin and his color was grey. How long had he looked like this? How come I did not see it before now? Again and again, I would beat myself up for my negligence. Had I been so preoccupied with the kids and the renovations that I neglected to see what was right in front of me?

I hated to leave him. He was so tired. But my sitter needed to go home and my children needed me. I rarely left my children. They were used to having their mommy home with them and a daddy who came home from work every night. In the morning when I left for the hospital, my little daughter Gilly clung to my legs and begged me not to leave her. Cullen was asking questions about the hospital and he wanted to know when his daddy would be coming home. I needed to be with Fred but my children needed me too. I could not stay any longer. I kissed Fred. "Sleep well my darling. I will see you in the morning." There was so much that was left unsaid.

"Call me when you get home. I need to know you are home safe." He held my hand as I lingered at the bedside.

"Will do." I blew him a kiss as I turned and left the room. I know he saw the tears in my eyes as one escaped and trickled down my cheek.

I did my best to walk in the light and not give into the dark whisperings in my head. I rationalized and intellectualized as I tried to make sense of what had happened in the last few days. I played the litany of platitudes over and over in my head: he is a young man, he takes good care of himself, Henry Ford Hospital is a world renown medical center, these people are on top of things, they are specialists in their fields, these are caring and compassionate people and they will take care of Fred, it could be anything, don't think the worst, Freddy will be okay and home with us soon. And when I would get to the end of the litany I would play it all over again. He is a young man, he takes good care of himself... and on and on and on as I tried to keep my demons at bay.

In my exhaustion I stopped at the grocery store before I went home. I picked up some milk and fruit and diapers. When I got home the children were already in bed. I went upstairs to kiss them good night and I took a moment to watch them sleep . . . my beautiful, beautiful children. The house was peaceful. I put the food away and then I started the laundry before I fell into bed. I am certain I was asleep before my feet were off the ground.

I woke to the hugs and snuggles of my little ones and the pressing needs of the day. Gilly needed her wet diaper changed and Cullen wanted to eat. And so the day began, just like so many other days . . .

Later in the morning, when I arrived at the hospital, Freddy is all cleaned up. He pats the bed for me to sit next to him. I snuggle in close and feel the warmth of his body. He enfolds me in his arms as we try not to disturb the IV. He has just started to speak when a doctor walks in. The red stitching of the coat indicates that this is Dr. Patrick Roberts, Internal Medicine. Oh, so this is Fred's internist.

They look at each other and then at me. Fred says, "I haven't had a chance to tell her yet."

"What? For God's sake, what?" My voice betrays the panic I feel. I look to Fred to answer me. "What?"

The doctor says, "I'll give you a few minutes alone," and he walks out.

I am frantic. What has happened? "I am so sorry, Honey. I have been up all night trying to figure out how to tell you this." He takes a breath, pauses and then begins, "The results of the bone marrow biopsy came back. I have a form of bone marrow cancer. Multiple myeloma."

My world collapses. I feel like my heart is being ripped out of my body.

"No. It cannot be."

Fred continues. He gives me the details rather quickly because he wants me to hear this from him and he knows that Dr. Roberts waits outside the door to give us more of the specifics. Fred says that he is in the fourth of four stages and they think he has about three months to live.

He holds me as I cry uncontrollably. He whispers, "I am so sorry, I'm so sorry." He is contrite as if somehow he willingly chose this and that he has broken a promise and it is breaking his heart. "Maybe you can move back with your parents and they can help you raise the kids."

"No! No! Stop talking like this. Who told you this?" This is moving all too quickly. I cannot comprehend it. Fred slows down and gives me a moment to try to catch up, to try and understand. I am completely unprepared. In the last few days I had tip-toed around the idea that Fred might be sick but I was toying with the notion of some type of chronic condition, not a fatal illness. I am completely blindsided. The thought of losing my beloved Freddy fills me with terror, for I know that this is a loss from which I may never recover.

As I cry, Fred tells me what transpired since last night. Apparently about 11:00 pm, long after I had left for home, some doctor that Fred had never laid eyes on came to his room where he was alone and told him, "Get your affairs in order; you have about three months to live," and then he walked out.

Fred has been lying awake all night trying to figure out how to tell me this and he was mentally making arrangements to take care of the kids and me. His concerns are not for himself but for his family.

I am outraged that my beloved husband has been delivered a death sentence without the benefit of some human compassion. I am outraged at the audacity of this doctor who thinks he is clairvoyant and that he knows what God's plan for my beloved is.

There is a knock on the door and Dr. Roberts re-enters the room. "The results of the bone marrow biopsy indicate that Fred has multiple myeloma. Plasma cells help the body's immune system fight disease by producing antibodies. In multiple myeloma, the plasma cells grow out of control and form tumors in the bone marrow. The excess growth of plasma cells interferes with the body's ability to make red blood cells, white blood cells and platelets. This leads to an increase in infections and abnormal bleeding. The cancer cells growing in the bone marrow can cause pain and destruction of the bones. It is a very rare form of cancer. This cancer usually affects the elderly and predominantly males of African descent."

Is this guy for real? It sounds like he has memorized the textbook. He speaks rapidly and throws around the medical vernacular, so he will appear all knowing. I have seen this so many times before. This is a common ploy used by doctors to distance themselves from their patients and their humanity, their fears and their sadness. This tactic is used to discourage questions.

I launch into my question anyway, "What can be done?" I can barely get the words out.

"The oncologist, Dr. Magno will be in later today to discuss the treatment options." I get nothing from him because he does not know. "I am so sorry." He sounds like he is making a condolence call and I am not having any of it.

My mind is racing. This is Fred's internist and the asshole who delivered the death sentence was his partner, Dr. Paris. This is the doctor who was too busy to see him last Tuesday when he had a raging fever and a bloody nose. This is the doctor who has been prescribing course after course of antibiotics for the last year but never thought to do some blood work. I am angry. He says he is sorry but how about owning up to the fact that he missed the diagnosis. He does not accept any responsibility for that. Now he wants permission to coordinate Fred's care and work with the oncologist. Oh, I think not.

I can hardly speak. I do not trust myself to keep a civil tongue. Dr. Roberts drops his head and mumbles another, "I am sorry," as he leaves the room. He can't get out of here fast enough.

Fred is forgiving. I, on the other hand, have much to learn about forgiveness. Fred is exhausted and needs to sleep. I lie next to him, and he is asleep in a matter of moments. I know how uncomfortable the nursing staff feels when people sit on the patient's bed, let alone lie in it, but I could not care less. I know Fred needs me with him now.

In this quiet moment I beg God for help. Please Dear God, not this ...please, oh please... do not test me like this. I have tried to be your obedient daughter and I know that I have faltered and failed repeatedly but please not this. Fred has embraced you and loves you. He loves you and he loves his life. How dare you be so cruel as to bless us with real love and happiness and then rip it away from us? You know my children need their father. You sent your son to earth but you did not ask Mary to be a single mother. No, you gave her a husband and an earthly father for Jesus. How dare you ask this of me? I cannot go on without him. How could you possibly need him more than I do? More than his children do? Please God, not now, not yet.

The tears run freely down my hot red face. My heart pumps rapidly in my chest and the more I try to negotiate with God the more rapid my breathing becomes. I know

I need to stop this as I am beginning to hyperventilate. I place my hands over my nose and mouth and try to regain some self-control. As my breathing slows I offer up one more thought to God…this is not over yet, I am so not finished talking to you about this.

As Fred sleeps on, I grab The Bible from the bedside table. Let's just see what God has to say about this. I am not a scripture scholar and I have no idea where to begin. So I close my eyes and ask for guidance…Just what do you have to say about this?

I open The Bible to Luke 7:11-17

Soon afterward, Jesus went to a town called Nain, and his disciples and a large crowd went along with him. As he approached the town gate, a dead person was carried out—the only son of his mother, and she was a widow. And a large crowd from the town was with her. When the Lord saw her, his heart went out to her and he said, "Don't cry." Then he went up and touched the coffin, and those carrying it stood still. He said, "Young man, I say to you, get up!" The dead man sat up and began to talk, and Jesus gave him back to his mother. They were all filled with awe and praised God. "A great prophet has appeared among us," they said. "God has come to help his people." This news about Jesus spread throughout Judea and the surrounding country.
–Luke 7:11-17

When you reduce this story down to its bare essentials, it comes down to two people: Jesus, coming into town, and a weeping, heartbroken widow leading the procession that bears her dead son to his final resting place. Just two people, not even a prayer uttered, and compassion touches the heart of God's Son and the miracle was granted.

This was not lost on me. I believe this scripture verse was an answer to my prayer. God is compassionate. I put my faith in this answer rather than the prognosis of the doctor who portrayed himself as all knowing.

I read the passage again and then closed the Bible and put it back on the stand. I was awe struck and filled with a holy stillness. I offered up a simple prayer of gratitude...Thank you God for hearing me.

The scriptures spoke of a miracle and I believe in miracles...Grandma's death had been nothing short of miraculous. She had stepped through to the other side and I had witnessed it. This was not the kind of miracle I sought. I wanted my life back the way it was. I did not want to let go of it. I just wanted God to fix my world. I wanted Fred to be healed and well.

When Fred awoke, we began the painful business of informing the family of the diagnosis. Fred was so ill that this responsibility was delegated to me. I made calls from the payphone near the nurse's station. I could hardly get the words out without dissolving into tears. I held tight to the promises made and the answers given. I prayed unceasingly.

I have often said that faith is a gift and I know that I have been blessed with the gift of faith. In this moment I was clinging to my faith with all the strength that my very fragile spirit could muster, but the other reality rests in my humanity and that world was collapsing.

The day was like a bad dream, and the sequence and the details have become all muddled, but I do remember that Fred's parents came to the hospital with Shelley and Joel. Privately, I was chastised for being so emotional around Fred. They made it clear that I must try to be optimistic or at least try to put on a good face in Fred's presence. I tried but I was so profoundly afraid and devastated; they had not talked to the doctor and they did not hear the dire prognosis.

Joel accompanied me to the cafeteria, as I had been unable to eat for days. I was forgetful and confused. There in the cafeteria I put my head down on the table and cried. I was inconsolable. Joel sat silently with me while I cried and eventually my tears subsided and I was able to explain to him what the doctor had told us. He just stayed with me and listened and when I had nothing left to say he let me know that he would help the family understand. In the interim, Fred was fielding phone calls from well-meaning friends. They promised him far more than they were capable of delivering.

I called my dear friend Jill. I don't recall what I told her but the next thing I knew one of the nurses was tapping me on the shoulder to let me know that Jill had come to the hospital and was in the waiting room. I was visibly shaken when I saw her so there and then she enfolded me in her arms like a mother. She held me while I cried. Her very presence fortified me and this gesture of love would forever cement the bonds of our friendship. I returned to Fred after I had washed away my tears.

I walked back into the room and saw him looking frail and vulnerable against the stark white sheets of the hospital bed.

I sat beside him on the bed and held his hands in mine, "Fred, we need to make a plan. We can either agree to give our power over to the doctors or we can make a decision to fight and hold onto this life with all the strength that we can possibly muster. I am unwilling to let you go."

"Oh Jeanne and I am unwilling to go." One small tear rolled down his cheek as he swallowed hard in an effort to keep the floodgates from spilling over.

"While you were sleeping I had a little heart to heart with God." I leaned in and kissed away the lone tear.

"Go on." He looked me in the eye and nodded.

"Well, I asked for help and in my heart I know I was led to read the Bible." I reach over and pick up the Bible from the bedside table. "I opened the Bible to this particular passage."

And I read aloud the passage from Luke 7:11-17.

"I know that this is an enormous test of faith but I believe that this is the answer to a prayer, and the answer is clear. God will save you. Please, let us try with all of our strength to put our faith and trust in God. I will help you in any and every way I can but you and I need to treat this illness with all the tools that are available to us and not give up, as I cannot bear to lose you."

"I cannot bear to lose you either. If you want to fight this, count me in."

I think it was in this moment that we were transformed. We no longer saw ourselves as victims of some tragic injustice but rather as people who could and would endure this hardship and embrace our time and our life together.

I regained a bit of composure as I prepared to go to battle to protect and care for my beloved husband and my family. Fred was desperately ill and he looked to me to help him through the maze of medical jargon and all the decisions that needed to be faced in the weeks to come. I would speak for Fred when he was too ill or too tired. I asked the questions that needed to be asked and pushed for answers when they were not forth coming. I do not know where the strength came from but come it did. So Fred and I, with the support of our family and friends, battled to hold onto his life.

Dr. Magno, the oncologist met with us to discuss the treatment options. We both really liked him. Unlike the two internists, he provided us with hope; the plan was to treat Fred aggressively and prolong his life. He was also unwilling to discuss Fred's prognosis because he recognized that each person is different. This disease may behave differently in Fred than it did in others and Fred's response to the treatment would be as individual as he was.

He offered Fred the option to have his back irradiated. This would be strictly for pain control but it could cause the malignant cells to migrate and become more aggressive somewhere else. We looked to one another and decided in an instant that we were in this for a cure and were not interested in short-term solutions that might diminish his chances of long-term survival. In the end we decided that Fred would continue to receive antibiotics for his pneumonia, as well as blood transfusions prior to starting chemotherapy.

At this time Fred's platelets were so low that if he started bleeding they might not be able to get the bleeding to stop. The doctors decided to go to the operating room to put in a central line to draw blood, and to inject medication. They did the procedure under a local anesthetic while Fred was awake.

After the procedure Fred confided to me that the doctor was freaking out in the OR. Fred had to tell him that he was doing fine, but the doc was sweating profusely and letting go with a few expletives as things clearly were not going as planned. Fred reassured him all through the procedure, "I have no intention of checking out today."

The doctor told me later, "I nearly lost him in the OR."

Later Fred reassured me, "Not a chance, the doc was just a kid and just needed a bit more confidence."

The doc shook Fred's hand as he told me, "He is one in a million." I already knew.

Chemotherapy was planned to begin on Monday but first we needed to give our informed consent. The chemotherapy was known to cause many side effects, including severe birth defects, so we were required to sign documents saying we would practice birth control. But I don't remember any discussion of the chemo leading to sterility and I did not have the presence of mind to ask. Fred and I had wanted another child. But in this moment we were not thinking about another baby. I was only concerned about saving my husband and taking care of the two children that we already had. Later I would feel differently as I would never have another child.

Fred tolerated the first round of chemotherapy pretty well. In the interim I met with the home care people. Since I am a Registered Nurse, Fred would not need home care. I would care for him at home. We were so ready to go home.

The kids were so happy to see their Daddy. Fred was brought to tears at the sight of them. They had missed one another badly. They climbed all over him, asked a million questions before they would settle in on his lap for a snuggle. His lap was their throne and they were the prince and princess of our kingdom. They knew that their Daddy was sick, but we did not elaborate, as Cullen was only 4 and Gillian 18 months old.

I consciously chose not to look too far down this road, for the future terrified me. I did not want to know where this path would lead. I reflect back on the wisdom of the geneticist who asked if we were really ready to embrace life with all that is unknown and unknowable. My answer was and is still yes. I asked God again to grant me another day and the strength not to give into fear and despair. The nagging question rattled me despite my best efforts to silence it: will my children grow to know their father? I tried my best to stay grounded in the present, but inside I was as fragile as a porcelain doll.

The chemo had weakened Fred terribly. The chemotherapy attacks rapidly dividing cells, and this is what malignant cells do: divide rapidly. Hair cells and the cells in the entire intestinal tract also divide rapidly so they are also affected by the chemotherapy. Fred was unable to eat as he had sores in his mouth and down his throat. He was nauseated. I tried to coax him to eat but he could not, and thus he grew weaker and weaker by the day.

Death camped at our doorstep. I had seen through the veil to the spiritual world when Gram was dying. It broke my heart to lose her but she was 87 years old. All deaths are sad for the people left behind but to lose someone who is young and in the prime of their life . . . that is tragic. I know that eternity and the spirit world are just a breath away for all of us and yet I was afraid and ill-prepared to lose my husband. Help me God for I am losing my grasp.

I took the children to church with me, as it was Palm Sunday. I prayed for healing for my beloved husband. I need him, and my children need their father. I was making my very best effort to be a good Catholic daughter and for good Catholics, Sunday Mass is obligatory. Since Fred had been sick, these past three weeks, I was making good on all my promises to God. I was dotting my I's and crossing my T's to make certain that I fulfilled my half of the agreement. However, when the children and I arrived at home after Mass, I found Fred lying on the bathroom floor. He had fallen and he was too weak to get up. I chastised myself for deciding to go to Mass.

Fred, forgive me. I am so sorry. God, I am sorry, so sorry. I should have known better. I see now how I was using my attendance at Mass as a way to control you. I wanted to be certain that you kept up your end of the bargain. If I am the devoted Catholic daughter then you must grant Fred healing and prolong his life. This is not faith. This is my attempt to control God. Good luck with that, Jeanne. This is not what you need or want from me. I know that you do not need me on my knees, throwing money into the collection plate, and reciting prayers and singing your praises in a church full of well-dressed people. Today of all days when the readings are of the crucifixion of your son, where we hear of the disciples denying Jesus and abandoning him in his time of need, I find my husband abandoned by me, his wife, and lying on the floor of the bathroom. Now, how clearly I see that I am needed here with Fred. He needs me to be at home with him, to care for him. God does not need me fulfilling some obligation imposed by the church. Not now, this is wrong . . . just wrong . . . I need to get my fucking head on straight and start listening to my heart and doing what I know is right. God would not care, and does not care if I am at Mass or not. I am needed at home. Oh God, I am so sorry. God, forgive me for I know not what I do . . . Freddy, forgive me.

CHAPTER 6

The Path

In the weeks to come Fred and I would find a way to live on this very fine line that kept us on the edge of eternity. His health was fragile and we both knew this. We grew closer to one another and held on tight to the life we had built. We wove together the elements of our faith until we felt strengthened to meet the challenges that lie ahead.

One morning while I was changing the bandages on Fred's chest and clearing the IV tubing, tears began to well up in my eyes and roll silently down my face. Fred was so thin and the chest wound was so raw and only just beginning to heal. I was thinking; Is this part of some grand design? Is this why I became a nurse? In his gentle way Fred took my face in his hands and kissed my tears away. "Honey, you look so sad and it breaks my heart to see you like this." I grabbed a tissue and tried to catch the tears as they fell. "Please don't mourn me while I'm here."

In that moment I had an awakening. Fred's words stopped me. I now saw clearly that if I kept this up, I would miss this time we had together. "I promise you I will stop right now."

I solemnly vowed to do my best. He was here now and I would do my best to stay in the present. I did not want to give this precious time away.

I promised myself that I would do my best to stop crying in the presence of my family. How could I expect Fred to be strong if I was falling apart all the time? Years later I would come to see, that perhaps this was what Fred's family had been asking of me when they admonished me for being so despondent when Fred was first diagnosed.

As we sat on the bed amidst the medical paraphernalia we made some very important decisions. There would be no more talk of dying. We agreed that there is living and there is dead. While we are on this earth there is only living and in that moment we made a conscious choice to make the most of each and every day.

We talked about my Grandma. I recounted a memory I carry of her, "Gram once told me that her favorite time of her life was when she had her family at home." I made a deliberate decision not to waste this time. "If this is to be the best time of our lives then we need to be certain that we don't miss it."

Fred and I both believe in a life after death. We both know, all too well that the body will age and die but we believe that the soul is eternal. So death is just a transition for the soul to another form of existence. We also believe in a God that loves us. The proof being that every day we marvel at the wonders of creation and that we are still astounded that we have found one another and have been blessed with two beautiful children. Fred and I have discussed it and are in agreement that we don't know where the soul goes when the body dies. Some people call it heaven. What will heaven be like? I certainly do not know and I choose not to spend any time thinking about it. When I worry, I am not trusting My Creator . . . but I do, and so does Fred.

It is God that gives life and it is God that will decide the moment of our soul's transition. If one believes that there is life after death and that death is just the release of the soul to eternal life, then eternity is just part of this continuum that we are living in right now.

Why waste this beautiful moment? We consciously decided not to. In talking with one another, our souls' connection became even stronger and we found a way to a peaceful acceptance of our situation.

We made the decision to live every day, as we don't know how much time we will have. But, neither does anyone else.

I reflect on the parable of the ten bridesmaids . . .

Watch therefore, for you know neither the day nor the hour in which the Son of Man is coming

– Matthew 25:13

I choose to think this means that we don't know when Jesus will be coming for us to help our souls cross over.

Living in the present requires a conscious effort, but with practice I found it was not as difficult as I thought it would be. When I find myself worrying about something that may or may not happen, I stop and refocus my attention on what is happening now.

However, the ups and downs of life have exhausted me and I was often asleep before my feet were off the ground. It is staying asleep that is difficult for me. Once again I awoke in the dark. Fred was lying close to me and I found comfort in the warmth of his body, and listened to his rhythmic breathing with the hope that his breathing would lull me back to sleep. But sleep eluded me and my mind began to wander.

Again I was confronting God. How could this have happened to me? To us? And again there is no response to the questions I have so succinctly asked. I offered up my defense. I am a good girl. I am the one who does the right thing, over and over and over again. Yes, I know I have made some mistakes but when push comes to shove, I do the right thing. I don't deserve this. I am the good girl who has played by the rules. I thought I was one of the favored ones. Fred has always been the golden boy. He does not deserve this. Is this some kind of Divine retribution? If so what could Fred or I possibly have done to deserve this? Why are we being made to suffer? And still no answer.

And yet somehow through the long and lonely night I gained a modicum of clarity: perhaps this is not how the spiritual world works. If God's grace is unearned, and his kindness, blessings and mercies are undeserved, then perhaps when things go badly in one's life, it is not Divine retribution.

Maybe it just is.

Maybe difficult times are a test for the spirit. A test to determine how you will deal with the life that you have been given.

Will you learn what you need to learn for the growth and perfection of your soul?

The questions remain unanswered.

Eventually sleep would overcome me as I found a sense of peace in the understanding that God has not abandoned us and was not punishing us and perhaps we had not fallen from grace.

Our dear friends Dan and Linda Silvasi came to our aid. Dan is an anesthesiologist. When he learned of Fred's illness he took it upon himself to do the research and find the best place and the best doctor for a second opinion. He determined who was doing the cutting edge research on multiple myeloma, and helped Fred get an appointment with Dr. Robert Kyle at the Mayo Clinic in Rochester, Minnesota.

We went to the Mayo Clinic the week before Easter. Fred was dreadfully weak. The first day we met with Dr. Kyle, and he ordered a plethora of tests: additional blood and urine testing, x-rays and another bone marrow biopsy. After the testing was completed, that evening we went out for dinner in the Mayo Clinic complex. The complex is like a small city unto itself. After dinner, Fred wanted to go shopping for my birthday. At his insistence I purchased a beautiful black dress with an ivory lace collar, there was a nagging intrusion that this would be the dress I would wear to Fred's funeral. I struggled to push the thoughts away.

The following morning Fred's back pain was so severe that he could not stand, he could not bear his own weight. He went to his appointments in a wheel chair and they ordered an MRI only to determine that his spinal column was deteriorating from the disease.

The bone marrow tumors had left his vertebrae riddled with small holes, as if it had been moth eaten. They measured him and he had lost nearly 4 inches of height in about 5 weeks. This was the cause of his back pain.

Dr. Kyle confirmed the diagnosis and he reassured us that the people at Ford Hospital were using the most current treatment protocol and that given Fred's age he might be a candidate for a bone marrow transplant. He gave us a bit of hope when he told us that he actually knew of one person who had survived this disease. This was the first time we had heard this from anyone, and yet this was enough to hold on to. Fred was determined that he would be the next survivor. After all, he was certain that no one had more of a reason to live than he had.

On our flight home we were upgraded to first class as Fred was unable to get the wheelchair down the aisle of the plane and he was unable to walk. He was in agony from the back pain when Shelley and Joel picked us up at the airport. It was Saturday night and the next day would be Easter Sunday. Instead of going home we went directly to the emergency room at Henry Ford Hospital. Fred was hurting and running a fever. He should have been admitted directly to the hospital but because of an administrative snafu, instead he sat in the ER on a gurney. The place was a madhouse, with all types of people with all kinds of problems.

Fred's ability to fight infection was severely compromised by the chemotherapy and they were dilly-dicking around while people were spreading their disease and pestilence. After an intolerable wait, a medical student in a short white coat came in to examine Fred.

"Good Evening Mr." he looked down at the chart, "Miller, I am Dr. So and So, what brings you in tonight?"

Fred was too ill to answer so I answered for him. "My husband has been recently diagnosed with multiple myeloma. We have just spent the week at the Mayo Clinic. He was able to walk on Wednesday and now his pain is so severe he can no longer stand as the disease has invaded his spinal column."

"Why is he wearing the mask? Is he contagious?" He looked fearful as if he might catch leprosy by being in the same room with Fred.

"No, his immune system is compromised from the chemotherapy. He is not a danger to you or anyone but being here with sick people is dangerous for him....that is the reason for the mask."

I bit my tongue while he asked a multitude of stupid, irrelevant questions. Fred was too ill and short of breath to answer, but when this medical student began to do a neurological exam on my husband who could not walk, and he neglected to take Fred's shoes off, I lost my fucking mind.

"Get out of here! Do not touch my husband. He is sick and you are not a doctor. Do you have a license to practice medicine? We both know that you do not. I'll be damned if you are going to practice on my husband." Fred was too tired and too ill to object. He laid his head back on the pillow and used his arms to shield his eyes from the florescent lights and probably to get some distance from his crazy wife.

I stormed into the hallway and picked up the house phone labeled "For Physician Use Only" and I paged Fred's oncologist. Within moments I heard the operator on the overhead speaker paging Dr. Magno to the phone I was calling from. When Dr. Magno called back, I explained our situation and Fred was out of the ER and admitted post haste . . . a bit unorthodox but it worked.

I have been known to be the mother bear. Do not mess with my loved ones or I will scratch your eyes out.

WWJD. What Would Jesus Do? Not exactly this. I was not patient and I was not long suffering and I am not particularly proud of my behavior. I am a red head and have the notorious accompanying temper. I have spent my entire life trying to keep it under my control. This night I was not successful. I have a long fuse but when the powder keg blows, watch out! The stories from this night live on and on.

The next day was Easter Sunday. My little children were expecting the Easter Bunny. I had nothing prepared, as the last few weeks had been a nightmare as I watched my life unravel. On the way home from the hospital, Shelley and Joel stopped at an all night drug store but everything was picked over. I grabbed a few bags of jellybeans and Easter candy and figured I'd just have to make do.

When I arrived at home there were two boxes sitting on the front porch. Fred's friends, Howard and Phyllis from Colorado, had sent beautiful Easter baskets with age and gender appropriate gifts for the kids. I broke down and sobbed; somehow they knew exactly what was needed in this moment. I don't believe in coincidence.

Fred and I had made the decision that we are going to fight this. We would not give up our power to anyone, including the medical establishment. We heard the message from the internist loud and clear, "No survivors." We now knew that this was not true. Someone had survived. While we agreed to consider what the medical community was offering, we also began to explore some alternative healing strategies.

Fred and I are spiritual people. In this crisis, again and again we turned to God and spiritual healing. We believe that the spirit of God dwells within all of us. So through daily prayer we consciously tried to cultivate the gifts of the Holy Spirit: love, joy, peace, patience, kindness, goodness, faithfulness, gentleness and self- control. I was not always successful but I continued to persevere.

People use different defense mechanisms to help them cope in a crisis and I am certain that a psychiatrist would have a field day with me. But I am an avid reader and so I find comfort in what I refer to as bibliotherapy. A shrink might call it intellectualizing. Call it what you will but it works for me and so I read everything I could get my hands on that related to healing and passed only the best on to Fred. We found great wisdom in the writings of Dr. Bernie Siegel, Louise Hay, Norman Cousins and Deepak Chopra. To try to include a synopsis of what we learned and began to practice in our lives, cannot begin to do justice to the contribution these people made to Fred's healing, but I will try to help you see the shift that was taking place in Fred because of his willingness to see his disease as an opportunity to grow in love.

One of the first books that we read was given to Fred by his oncologist, Dr. Magno; it was <u>Love, Medicine and</u>

<u>Miracles</u> written by Dr. Bernie Siegel. Dr. Siegel wrote about exceptional cancer patients. These were people who lived longer than they had been expected to live. His research indicated that these survivors paid close attention to their feelings, expressed their emotions and made wise choices, and in doing so they became more spiritual and their bodies benefited.

Dr. Siegel also wrote about the physiology of optimism, and his work cites countless examples where optimism played a role in his patients return to health and healing. But one of the strongest recommendations he makes is to surrender your worry and fear and pain to God. By letting God deal with these very difficult things, one is free to use his or her time and energy on love, hope and joy. I think Fred needed permission to let go and let God. I know that I did. Once we relinquished the need to control that which was always beyond our control and always was in God's hands, it did indeed free both Fred and I to live this life in light and love.

Father Edward Farrell was the weekend priest at our parish and he taught a class that Fred elected to participate in. This class provided Fred a Catholic perspective on walking his own journey with God in a way that he could embrace. Father Farrell's work recognized the individuality of each of us and focused on how each of us is the embodiment of our own individual facet of God's glory, because the Spirit of God lives in each of us. The resounding conclusion is that we are holy vessels of the Spirit. I think Fred was comforted to find a teacher and a priest within our church that validated his understanding of God.

Louise Hay's work was also enormously helpful. Her work clarified and sharpened Fred's understanding that our thoughts matter, as do the words that we speak, for it is through our thoughts and our words that we create the experiences of our lives. Therefore, if we want to live in peace, harmony and balance, then we must first create these in our minds so that they may be manifested in our lives.

Fred's illness opened up some time for us. He was too ill to go to work so he was home with me and the children. Yes he was sick but we changed the way we looked at it, our perspective changed and we began to see this time that we had together as a gift. As our children played at our feet, we had time and opportunity to discuss what we had learned through these writings.

We began to pray aloud together every evening when we would get into bed. We would begin by addressing Our Creator by one of the myriad of names that recognized the awe we felt by being in the presence of the majestic spirit we know as God. Fred would usually start as we held hands in the dark and expressed our heart-felt gratitude for the blessings of the day and our ability to take part in them. Sometimes this was enough: a prayer of gratitude. Sometimes we would acknowledge our fears and ask for help. We learned quickly not to be too specific about how that help should be manifested in our lives, for we both knew, all too well, that God's ways are not our ways.

Fred's sense of peace was magnified each time he found another intellectual and spiritual guide that he could embrace and who would lead him further along on this path. His sense of well-being was enhanced as he was able to share what he was learning with those of us who were blessed to be in his presence.

Another thing we learned along the way, from the writings of Norman Cousins, is that humor and laughter create positive vibrations and healing energy. So we would regularly take some time to watch funny movies, share Far Side comics, and hang out with friends and our kids who provided us an ongoing source of comic relief.

Fred also started on a macrobiotic diet. A macrobiotic diet emphasizes eating whole grains, vegetables, beans and soy-based foods. It is low in saturated fats, meat, dairy, sugar and all processed foods. Fred embraced the diet whole-heartedly and I was willing to cook whatever Fred felt that he needed. But unlike most Americans, before he got sick. Fred was already thin at 6' 2" and 160 pounds. He was tall and lean and could always eat mountains of food. His weight plummeted rapidly and continuously with each round of chemo. The chemotherapy led to nausea, mouth sores and lack of appetite. Fred was unable to consume enough calories to maintain his weight. Within two months his weight had dropped to 135 pounds. He looked like a skeletal version of his former self, like a victim of a third world famine.

Both of our families spoke with me privately about the physical changes that were so obvious in Fred. Unanimously they agreed that the macrobiotic diet was a bad idea and chastised me for allowing Fred to continue on the diet and assisting him to do so by purchasing and preparing the food for him.

Later that spring Fred had been readmitted to the hospital for yet another bout of pneumonia. I was preparing his macrobiotic foods at home and bringing this food to the hospital every day. One afternoon the registered dietician paid us a visit in Fred's room.

This woman was about my age, in her early thirties, and about my height 5'6", but that was where the similarities ended. She must have weighed 350 lbs if she weighed an ounce. She was not exactly the role model for healthy eating and healthy lifestyle but with very little introduction about who she was or why she was there, she let both of us have it. "What do you think you are doing bringing him this food? You are a nurse? You obviously don't know anything about health and healing. Your husband is sick and will never get better on this kind of diet. He needs his protein and calories. This is a diet for kooks! You must be a kook!" and then she turned her wrath on Fred. "Do you have some kind of a death wish because this diet will kill you," and with that she blew out of the room like a storm.

I was speechless but Freddy started to laugh. "Poor dear, she means well. Does she really think she is in the position to be offering anyone advice on good nutrition? Perhaps I should go on a diet of Twinkies and Cheetos to prolong my life." In that moment, I let my anger and outrage drift away and I saw what Fred already knew: This poor woman was trying to exert her authority in an arena where she clearly was powerless.

Within a few minutes she walked back in the room and offered up an apology to Fred. He graciously accepted her apology, "Please, don't worry about it. We're okay," he reassured her for he saw her as she was: another child of God. And then she turned her complete attention towards him and acted as if I was invisible as she tried to explain why she thought he should eat a balanced diet complete with meat, dairy, fruits and vegetables and grain every day. Fred listened politely and then before she left, he thanked her for her time and concern.

In hindsight I can see more clearly. I believe Fred's decision to try a macrobiotic diet was very good for him. It created a shift in attitude where he was more than a patient with cancer and certainly more than a victim, he reclaimed his right to decide for himself what he would and would not do. He began to make his own decisions and regain some control about how he was going to live his life. I was not going to try and control my husband. This had never been the kind of relationship that we had and I was not going to tell him what he could or could not do.

However, when his blood cholesterol dropped to 6, Dr. Magno told Fred he thought it was in his best interest to stop the diet and find a way to increase his caloric intake, and Fred chose to honor this recommendation.

Fred spent a good part of these days quietly resting and reading. Fred was peaceful and I was frenetic. In the ensuing years I have had some time to reread these books that we both read after Fred was first diagnosed. I see now how they guided and helped Fred come to this place of peace.

Deepak Chopra advises people to be aware of their mortality. He goes on to say that death stalks each of us every moment of our existence and that once you become aware of that, one's life becomes magical, because then one's priorities are not the same.

Even though Fred's physical appearance was altered and he appeared very ill, there was an inner light in him that had begun to glow more brightly. Those who have always loved him have always seen it but now it burned so brightly it could not be missed or dismissed by anyone.

There is mystery all around us. Fred and I walked the fine line between what was happening in our physical world as he fought to stay with us through the pain and suffering of his illness, the indignities bestowed upon him by the medical community, and the loving embrace of his family and friends, and yet just *a breath away* the spiritual world awaits and exists in parallel. We did our best not to live in fear. We talked extensively about what we know and what at this time remains unknowable about the other side of the veil.

Fred and I walked the path between the two worlds. I cannot speak for Fred but I know that some days I walked in the light of the spirit and many other days all I could focus on were the realities of this world: a sick husband and the needs of two little kids.

What exactly is a spiritual journey?

Some have described it like a labyrinth where, once one enters the path, it will lead inward towards greater self knowledge and knowledge of the Divine. I am not certain that this analogy works for me.

I see the spiritual journey more like a hike that ultimately leads to a mountaintop with a beautiful vista that is often unseen while walking through the trees. As in hiking, there are times when one may catch a glimpse of the vista, and the path is clear and the route unencumbered, and the hiking is easy, and there a other times when the path is hidden or one may become distracted and lose the way.

The word journey originates in the 16th century from the French and means a daily travel. I find it interesting that many spiritual practices recommend daily practice, and I can clearly see the benefits of this kind of discipline.

However, the daily demands of my life provided frequent distraction and thus I was, and still am, often off the path and lost. And thus, my progress is slow. The world of the spirit continues whether I am paying attention or not.

I have heard the wisdom of the sages say, "Be still and know." But my life does not always allow for stillness. Some days my practice is better than others, some days I falter and some days I do not practice at all.

At this time, all I could do was deepen my vow to stay connected to Fred.

Brother, let me be your servant.
Let me be as Christ to you
Pray that I may have the grace
To let you be my servant, too
-Richard Gillard

It was my turn to serve.
It was my time to serve.

128

CHAPTER 7

The Dance of Life
Two Steps Forward
and
One Step Back

Summer 1991 to Fall 1992

A king size bed can be a beautiful thing for many reasons. Ours served a variety of purposes and all of them were good.

It was a Saturday morning in June and the kids were playing in our bedroom. They had been climbing on and off the bed all morning as they snuggled in with us. Fred had completed yet another round of chemo and it was time for me to disconnect the infusion pump and flush the IV lines. Cullen and Gillian were sitting on the bed watching. We had done our best not to frighten the kids about Fred's illness but Cullen was 4 years old and very curious. He had dozens of questions.

"Daddy, what is in your little purse?" Cullen asked as he pointed to the navy bag that was belted around Fred's waist and held the chemo infusion pump.

"This is the pump that pushes medicine into my chest," Fred explained as he showed Cullen where the lines from the pump attached to his chest tubes.

"I don't have any of those tubes on my tummy," Cullen stated as a matter of fact. "And neither does Gilly." He pulled up her pajama top and took a look, just to be sure.

"Does it hurt you Daddy, when they stick those needles in you?" His little face registered concern.

"No honey. It doesn't hurt. The needles go into the tubes and that doesn't hurt." Fred was patient and reassuring as both of the kids checked out the apparatus coming out of his chest. "This is how the doctors want Mommy to give me the magic medicine that is going to help me get better. It goes right in these tubes and then into my blood and then on to my heart where my heart will pump the medicine where it needs to go to work its magic." Fred's explanation seemed to satisfy Cullen's need for information.

The kids sat very still and watched while I disconnected the pump, wiped both ports down with alcohol and then flushed the lines with saline. As I gathered up the medical paraphernalia the kids claimed their rightful spots, one tucked underneath each of their Daddy's arms. "Come on in here. Now these…" Fred said as he picked up the two tubes that hung from his chest, "can also be used as microphones where you can sing songs right to my heart."

The kids didn't need any more encouragement than that as Cullen held onto the tubing and broke out into song,

"I've got that joy, joy, joy, joy
Down in my heart.
Down in my heart.
Down in my heart
and it's down in my heart to stay."
–George Willis Cooke

And as he started to repeat this refrain little Gilly took hold of the other tube and although she was not talking yet she hummed along and rocked her little blonde head back and forth in time with the music. She was not about to be left out of the fun, then or ever. This is one of the sweetest things I have ever seen and with tears in his eyes and a smile on his face Fred assured the kids, "I think this will really help me get better."

The three of them started to sing all kinds of little ditties as Fred joined in. He picked up one of the chest tubes and used it as a microphone and sang a song to Gilly that would become her theme song.

"When she smiles she makes the sunshine.
And fills the world with morning dew
Happiness runs in the family
She the girl from the good earth and the high tree forest
And she's just about the happiest girl that I ever knew
Yes she's just about the happiest girl that I ever knew."
–Matthews Southern Comfort

This concert to Fred's heart went on for the better part of an hour. They were all laughing and enjoying the moment. And so this became a family ritual; when each round of chemotherapy was completed, the kids sat with their Daddy and sang through the microphones to his heart.

Low and behold, Fred had a good response from the chemotherapy, his tumor load was decreasing and his health began to improve.

One morning Cullen came to get me from the bedroom. "Mommy, come into the kitchen; I have a surprise for you." He was still in his yellow footie pajamas as he took me by the hand and led me into the kitchen. "Daddy walked in here all by himself." Cullen and Fred were both beaming at me.

"Cully told me he thought it was time I tried to walk again. So I did." Fred said as he sat on a stool at the kitchen counter. We were all smiling then.

"How do you feel?" I asked tentatively. I know he did not want to disappoint any of us but I didn't want him to feel pushed to do anything he wasn't ready to.

"Pretty good. I've got a good coach here." Cullen moved in close to his Dad as he basked in the glory and praise. There was a unity between the two of them; it was as if they were two pieces of the same soul.

"I might be a little more comfortable on the couch." Fred conceded.

"Do you want me to get the wheelchair?" I offered, as it had been about 6 weeks since he had walked on his own.

"No, I think I can do it." I watched as he pressed his hands into his thighs, and slowly and carefully got to his feet and shuffled with baby steps into the living room. Cullen faced his Dad and backed out of the kitchen slowly, in front of his Daddy, in a supportive gesture that said you can do this but also I am here if you need me.

"You can do it Dad. Good job." He was sweet and encouraging and full of praise for his Daddy as he helped him to the couch. It was such a role reversal to see a four-year-old encourage his father with so much love. Cullen had been nurtured with love everyday of his life and when given an opportunity he returned that love to his father. My heart filled with joy as I watched this tender exchange.

Little by little Fred was getting better and stronger and we were full of hope.

It became a little easier to turn my thoughts away from the spiritual world and what awaited us beyond the veil. I did not want to dwell on that now so I put my time and attention into hanging on to Fred in this life. Clearly, he was needed here.

Fred received his chemo every 3 to 6 weeks depending upon his blood work. He qualified for an expensive new drug that increased his white cell counts. I gave him an injection in his buttocks nearly every day, and so he was able to get his chemo right on schedule.

We passed the dreaded three-month prognosis and, to everyone's surprise and delight, Fred was walking again, gaining weight, and feeling better. He had an amazing turn-around and within a couple of weeks he was strong enough to return to work.

I allowed myself to breathe and to believe that Fred may survive.

God is referred to by a myriad of names including *The Lord-Our Healer* (Exodus 15:26). This uncanny reversal in our fortune required me to pause and think. The Bible tells us that with God all things are possible. All things? Really? This is a matter of faith.

As I pondered these things an event occurred that I can only report-because I have no rational explanation.

Just after Gillian was born my mother's oldest sister, Sister Carol was diagnosed with breast cancer.

Sister Mary Carol Duffy was a member of the Sisters of the Presentation of the Blessed Virgin Mary in Dubuque, Iowa. In other words, she was a nun. She had been a teacher and lived in this community of women for over 50 years.

Sister Carol had gone to see her doctor for a routine annual exam and the doctor asked her about the results of her breast biopsy she was to have had the previous year. Sister Carol indicated that she had not had a breast biopsy and that this was the first indication she had that there was anything wrong. Apparently, there was a mass in her breast that was found during a routine mammogram and the results of her mammogram were filed away and she had never been notified. This was a year prior.

When the biopsy was finally done they determined that the tumor was malignant and the cancer had already metastasized to the other breast. There were people who encouraged Sister Carol to file a malpractice suit against the doctor but she would not hear of it. "People make mistakes. It is part of the human condition."

The sisters in her community prayed for her and she made the decision to undergo radiation and the tumors in both breasts completely disappeared. This was seen as miraculous at the time but two years later the cancer had returned and she was gravely ill.

Mom and I drove out to Iowa the weekend before she died to say good-bye to this lovely woman, Mom's sister and my aunt. The sisters gathered around her bedside. They had been praying around the clock for her. Her dearest friend, Sister Helen Marie, took me aside; she had something she needed to tell me. "Sister Carol has been praying that God take her and allow Fred to heal so that he can stay on earth to raise his family."

When she began to ask God for this in prayer, that was when Fred had begun to get better, and it was then that Sister Carol's tumors returned.

My heart broke open once again with love, gratitude and a profound sadness. She is the most Christ-like person I have ever known. Sister Carol died on Good Friday between 1 and 3 pm. The coincidence was not lost on me.

"No one shows greater love than when he lays down his life for his friends"
-John 15:13

I do not know what any of this means. But in the darkest of her days the spirit of this very holy human woman was asking God for favors and healing, not for herself but for my husband, and without ever expecting to be acknowledged or thanked in any way. As her body deteriorated, her spirit shone brightly.

We have been taught to believe that God hears our prayers. Is it possible that Sister Carol's life could be exchanged for Fred's? Had Sister Carol given Fred a gift? Is it possible to pass on your strength or blessing to someone else? I had witnessed a miracle when Gram died. And now this…if this was another miracle how would it be manifested?

Fred and I would send a large bleeding heart flower to be planted in the garden at the convent in memory of Sister Carol. The plant is perennial, it returns every spring and the flowers are pink and they look like a bleeding heart. We thought this would be apropos as a living memorial.

Later that spring two more gifts would appear.

After 18 months of chemotherapy Fred was feeling well and strong but the chemo he was prescribed is cardio toxic and can lead to heart failure so there was only so much of it that he could take. The doctors started to talk to Fred about a bone marrow transplant. There were a number of obstacles that needed to be addressed before a BMT could even be considered: Fred's insurance would have to be willing to pay for it and BMTs are very expensive, Fred would have to be healthy enough to undergo the transplant because BMTs can be brutal, and there would need to be a bone marrow match.

Fred went to work every day he possibly could. He worked so he would retain his insurance. Even if everything else were to come together, without insurance Fred could not have the transplant. The injustice of this makes me irate. Most insurance programs are tied to employment but if you become ill and cannot work, then to add insult to injury, not only do people lose their jobs but they also lose their health care coverage when they need it the most.

Although Fred's strength and stamina had increased greatly, from the low point when Fred was first diagnosed, those in our inner circle understood all too well that Fred must also get even stronger if he was to survive a bone marrow transplant. There were so many things that were beyond his control, but at this point and time, getting fit was not one of them.

One evening, we were sitting in the family room with Mom and Dad as we watched the kids building castles with blocks on the floor. Dinner was finished and the sun was about to set over the lake as we lingered. Dad took a breath and launched into a proposal, "Your mother and I challenge the two of you to a bike race to Minneapolis."

"What?" I asked, as this seemed ridiculous on so many fronts. "Minneapolis?"

"On the Life Cycle, you know the stationary bike." Dad smiled as Mom shook her head in a way that implied that she had already given her consent to yet another one of his crazy schemes.

"John, your brother, lives in Minneapolis, so that's the destination. " Mom explained as if somehow that legitimized this craziness.

Without a moment of hesitation Fred asked, "How far is it?"

"Only 630 miles from Detroit to Minneapolis. The rules are: both members of the team must ride and the first team to add 630 miles to their odometer wins. Are you in?" Dad had clearly thought through all the details.

I started to protest as I have engaged in these kinds of shenanigans with Dad all my life but before I could utter a word, Fred spoke up, "We are all in and we will kick your butts!"

I looked at the three of them as if they had lost their minds. I could not believe my ears. I was being dragged into another crazy, hair-brained idea yet again. But Fred and Dad's enthusiasm were so contagious that in the end I agreed to be a participant, albeit a reluctant one.

"Your bike has 1247 miles on it today and ours has 3545." Dad smiled and confessed, "I took the liberty of checking it out." I was not surprised by his admission.

So we logged our miles on our stationary bikes. Admittedly, Mom and I did not do our share but Fred and Dad are fierce competitors and they both wanted to win. Dad secretly checked the odometer on our bike when he was out at our house. Recognizing that we were ahead, Dad went home and rode day and night. In the end they beat us out of the prize.

In celebration of their victory, we took Mom and Dad out to dinner and Fred made an elaborate presentation of a trophy he had engraved in their honor. We laughed and enjoyed ourselves as we celebrated their victory, but although unspoken, the real celebration was about Fred's return to health.

When spring approached, Fred and Dad planned to surprise me with a new bike for Mother's Day. But when Dad arrived at our house, instead of one bike as they had planned, Dad had two new purple mountain bikes on the bike rack on the roof of his car, one for me and one for Fred.

When Fred figured out that one of the bikes was for him, he was moved to tears. As we stood in the driveway, Fred was choked up as he embraced me and whispered in my ear, "Your Dad thinks I'm going to survive or he would not have bought me this expensive bike."

Dad's belief in Fred lifted him up.

Fred rode that bike every day that summer. He rode places he had no business riding as he joined a group of men who went mountain biking. I had to bite my tongue when he arrived home from his weekly ride all banged up and dirty. We were all counting on Fred. He lived positively and it was infectious.

Another gift came to us every bit as welcome as Mom and Dad's gift of faith that Fred would be well again. If Fred were eligible for a bone marrow transplant he would need the gift of a bone marrow donor. In 1992, without a familial match, Fred's odds of finding a donor were at best one in twenty thousand to possibly one in one hundred thousand. Fred's siblings were the first to be tested. It would take a few weeks before anything definitive would be known.

One afternoon when we were both at home, Fred's sister Shelley called. She did not match. This was exceedingly hard for her, as she would have done anything to save her brother. Their love for one another ran very deep. Later the same day his brother, Kirk, called, "The good news is that Fred has a bone marrow donor, the bad news is that it's me."

Kirk is a Godsend. He is 15 years younger than Fred. He is a child of Fred's parents' unplanned pregnancy. Fred and Kirk's bone marrow matched: a perfect match. The transplant was scheduled for the fall 1992.

Fred learned a great deal from his illness. The circumstances of his life had taught him to live in the present. He valued his days and did not waste them. He was full of joy and had an unbridled exuberance for life and all that it had to offer. He took it upon himself to be kind, loving, generous and forgiving, for he knew that he was already living on borrowed time. Life is a great teacher if you are awake and pay attention. For those of us who were close to him, Fred had become our teacher and our guide. If Fred could find the joy and beauty in life, with all that he was facing, the rest of us had better learn to do the same.

The dark days and weeks ahead would challenge Fred, and all of us who loved him. The spiritual journey is not simply a path that weaves through our humanity and leads to God, for the path is not always straight and direct. Sometimes we move from the light where we feel secure and safe in the love and comfort of God's grace, but there are times when we are led into the darkness where we feel abandoned, afraid and alone. Where is God then? It is in this dark tunnel that our faith is challenged.

Don't forget in the darkness . . . what I showed you in the light.
-author unknown

Harper Hospital
October 1992
The Bone Marrow Transplant

We did our best to keep our demons at bay and so in our darkest hours we tried to count our blessings.

First of all it was an unfathomable gift that we were here at all. These people were the experts in this field. All the patients on the second floor were inmates in the bone marrow unit. The physicians and the nurses on the unit cared only for BMT patients. Fred was in a private room. Everyone was required to wash their hands in the vestibule before they entered and to put on a protective covering. This was to keep Fred from getting any illnesses while his immune system was so completely compromised by chemo and radiation. The children were not allowed on the floor, at all, as little children may be coming down with something and be totally unaware of it until they had already exposed other vulnerable people.

Fred would not be able to see our children for weeks. He had photographs of the kids and me in his room. He also had a poster of a marathon runner on the wall. The runner appeared to be running through the desert. Fred knew he was in for a long grueling run. The HEPA air filter ran continuously as the team of nurses instructed Fred and I in what to expect along with the long list of prohibitions. Life is precious and we understood the costs of trying to preserve it. We were in agreement if the BMT was Fred's best chance at long term survival...bring it on.

The second blessing was that Fred was ready: physically, intellectually, emotionally and spiritually. Preparation for the BMT included total body irradiation and 10 days of massive doses of chemotherapy to kill all of Fred's bone marrow, the source of his malignant cells.

The combination of chemo he received was excreted by the kidneys and thus was toxic to the bladder, so Fred had to wear an indwelling catheter for about 1 week in an effort to prevent injury to his bladder. Fred had been riding his mountain bike extensively in preparation for the BMT. He continued to ride the stationary bike everyday in the patients' sunroom, including the week when he wore a catheter and his urine was being collected in a bag. Fred soon received notoriety amongst the nurses and the other patients for being unbelievably tough and determined to get well.

The total body irradiation caused Fred to lose his thick, curly brown hair. It started to come out in clumps. It was the first time that Fred really looked like a cancer patient. It was hard for me to look at him and not see him as someone who was ill. We concurred that he would look better as Yul Brynner or Mr. Clean, so at his request I shaved off the remaining bits of his hair. He made a very handsome bald man and his quick wit returned as he found a whole variety of new ways to poke fun at himself.

The third blessing was that the donor was gifted to him long ago. Fred's brother Kirk was the donor. Fred's parents were willing to be open to God's plan and brought Kirk into the world, when his birth had been unplanned and inconvenient, as they were older when he was conceived and they thought that their family was already complete.

The doctors harvested the bone marrow from Kirk's hipbones while he was under general anesthesia. While Kirk was still in the recovery room, Fred's doctor was hanging the bag of bone marrow. They connected the tubing from the bag to the ports that led into Fred's chest. It looked just like any other blood transfusion. Fred's parents and his sister joined me at Fred's bedside and we all held our breath and prayed for both Fred and Kirk. Apparently, if all went according to the plan, Kirk's bone marrow cells would migrate to the marrow of Fred's bones and within a few days these cells would begin to produce healthy new blood cells for Fred.

I was overwhelmed with gratitude as I was absolutely convinced that my prayers and the prayers of countless others had been answered.

The fourth blessing was that Fred's spirit was amazingly strong. Within a few hours the side effects of the chemo and radiation began to rear their ugly heads as nausea and vomiting set in. Fred would vomit around the clock for 36 days. Although it was the last thing in the world he wanted to do, Fred needed to continue to eat. If he stopped eating they would connect him to total parenteral nutrition or TPN through one of the chest portals. Fred called it-mashed potatoes in a bag. He had talked with the other patients, and the word amongst the patients was that once they start you on the TPN that it was really difficult to get off of it and you could not go home until you could eat. Fred was determined to stay off the bag so he continued to eat, even though every time he ate anything he would vomit. Time stood still for he could not escape the misery. It was relentless. He said he was so dizzy that he felt like he had been spinning on a merry-go-round for weeks and he could not get off. The nausea, vomiting and diarrhea continued. He was plagued with intermittent fevers, restlessness and fatigue. And yet, he still put on a cheerful smile and joked with the doctors and nurses. He asked about their lives and their loved ones even when he was deathly ill. He won their hearts and they would visit him and care for him when I was needed at home, and I am eternally grateful for their loving presence.

Fred would meet with other patients in the sunroom when he was able. One afternoon he was visibly upset when he told me about another patient that he had become friends with. "This guy, Bob, owns a dry cleaner and he has insurance, it just isn't very good. His plan covers only part of the hospitalization, so he has to pick and choose which part of the treatment and medications he will take based on what they cost. He was saying he doesn't know if he can afford to survive because of all the meds he will need, if and when they ever let him out of here."

The reality of this was appalling to me. One did not have to look very far to see the injustices of this world. God help them. God help us all.

During this time, I felt myself drawn to those I love who had gone before me and yet seemed so especially close to me during this time. I prayed to Gram and to Sister Carol as we loved one another and still do.

I went to visit Fred every day and every day I prayed the rosary in the car. As I drove down the expressway I would beg Mary, as one mother to another, to see my situation and show mercy, and in compassion for my family, to intercede for me. I talked with her, as if she was sitting in the passenger seat and I asked her to consider how my children needed their father. "Jesus needed an earthly father and you needed a husband. God did not ask you to be a single mother. How can he ask this of me? Clearly I am ill equipped to raise these children without my husband.

144

Please, on my behalf, for the sake of my children, please help him to understand that I cannot do this alone. You are his mother, please, I beg you, and surely Jesus will listen to the pleas of his mother." I prayed the same prayers with the same intention every day during my commute to the hospital. I begged and pleaded for Divine mercy. I was that squeaky wheel. I was the sand in the shorts. I was irritating and I was without pride as I begged for help.

My Mother and Dad came to the house every day to be with my children. Gillian cried and clung to my legs and begged me not to leave her. She was three years old and by order of the BMT team she could not go to preschool for fear she would pick up an infection and I would transport it to the hospital. Cullen was in kindergarten at St. Hugo's, so he had some reprieve from the confines of home. He loved school and all his new friends. It was a good diversion for him. I, however, felt like I was juggling knives, trying to meet the needs of my family, and at any given moment the entire thing could come crashing down around me.

The kids talked to their Dad every night on the phone. Gillian always wanted to know what he had for dinner and the names of his nurses. Cullen and Fred chatted about the happenings in kindergarten and all the TV shows that his Dad got to watch because he was sick. Gilly wanted to know when her Daddy would be home from the "hostible."

During my daily visits to the hospital I would often take a nap with Fred. I was exhausted and I needed to be with him.

Fred's family would visit in the evenings and I would spend every night home with the children. I did my best to keep our home life as normal as possible, with the ever-present help of my devoted mother. The kids and I would have dinner together and then our bedtime rituals of baths and stacks of storybooks, followed by lullabies. I loved this time of night when I could snuggle with my children. I ended every night with a phone call to my beloved and then I would crawl into bed alone.

Forty-two days later Fred was released from the bone marrow unit. It was now mid- November. I brought candy to the nurses, as they had been amazing. They gave Fred a glorious send off. He was their Wünderkind. His was the second shortest stay on the unit. They counted Fred's success as a tribute to the care that they had provided, and well they should. They saw people in such dire straights that they rejoiced in the successes and wept tears of joy at the homecomings.

We were sent home with a box full of medication complete with instructions about what needed to be taken and when, there were instructions about foods that must be eaten and foods that were prohibited, how often we needed to check his temperature and his blood pressure. No animals, no house plants, no flowers, no Christmas tree, no raw vegetables, only fruit with thick skins that could be peeled away, no milk, no clothing that had been dry cleaned, no pepper, no dried herbs, and the list went on and on.

And no sex. Even though I had been talking to people on the other side about us…I would do anything to keep him here on this side with us. The prohibition on sex was not the big issue and so we promised to behave ourselves. The reality was that I just wanted to keep him alive.

We signed the instructions and were given all kinds of emergency phone numbers. Fred was required to return to the BMT outpatient department the very next day to have his blood drawn and to get a blood transfusion. He would need to go to the hospital every day for months and months but at least he would be home at night. We agreed to all the stipulations and signed the obligatory papers. I just wanted to bring my husband home.

When we arrived home, Mom was there with Gillian. Mom was always there. She helped me in any way and every way that she was able. My neighbor started calling her Saint Audrey, as she truly is an angel in human form. She does God's work in this world and with great humility.

Mom had cleaned the house and she and the kids had made and hung a "Welcome Home Daddy" banner on the front porch. Dinner was all made and ready for the oven.

Gillian had been sitting on the couch looking out the window and waiting for her Daddy for hours. That was a long time as she was only 3 years old.

Fred was swollen from the steroids. His hair was all gone from the radiation. His skin was yellow from the toxic levels of chemotherapy he had had to endure. Physically he was hardly recognizable as the same person. He wore a protective mask over his nose and mouth and a knit ski hat on his head when we walked in the house. He picked up Gillian at the door as he took off his mask, she pulled off his hat and rubbed his head and said, "Oh Daddy, the magic medicine has blown all your hair off!" We all laughed and cried tears of joy and relief that Fred was home. Gillian snuggled down on his lap and wanted him to tell her all about what happened at the "hostible."

When Cullen arrived home from school, he looked like a little man in his parochial school uniform complete with navy pants, light blue oxford cloth shirt and navy tie. He paused at the doorway to hang up his coat and put his backpack away. He was hesitant and a bit taken back by his Dad's appearance. Fred invited him to come and sit next to him on the couch. Fred put Cullen at ease with his loving and joking manner that Cullen had always known and so the visible changes in his Dad began to fade as Cullen reconnected with the unchanged essence of his well-loved father.

Mom had not seen Fred at the hospital. She had been helping us every day with the children at home. She loves Fred like a son but did not insert herself into our family homecoming even though she was welcome and had been invited to join us. She recognized that there would be time for her but that tonight Fred was ours. She made dinner and served us but stayed in the background and then headed for home, as we reconnected and re-united as a family.

The kids laughed, joked and played with their dad. We took them up for baths and bedtime stories. There was love and peace and joy in our home.

During my daily commutes back and forth from the hospital I had heard a song on the radio that touched my heart. I had purchased this new CD for Fred's homecoming. Once the children were asleep. I played it and invited him to dance with me in the family room. The music played in the background as we held one another and danced. We both cried tears of joy as our deepening love sustained us. Fred was home.

Beautiful in My Eyes
You're my peace of mind
in this crazy world
You're everything I've tried to find
Your love is pure
You're my rainbow skies
My only prayer is that you realize
you'll always be beautiful in my eyes
We won't say good-bye
cause true love never dies
You'll always be beautiful in my eyes
The passing years will show
that you will always grow
ever more beautiful in my eyes
–Joshua Kadison

CHAPTER 8

Ordinary Time

As Thanksgiving 1993 arrived, Fred was going to the hospital every day to have his blood drawn, his medications adjusted and his overall state of health monitored. In addition to everything else, he was also suffering from medication overload, something his doctors referred to as chemo toxicity. To add to the litany of maladies, somewhere along the line he had been infected with CMV or cyto meglic virus and he felt dreadful. IV antibiotics and anti viral medications were ordered and I infused the medications around the clock in our family room. We did everything in our power to keep Fred from being readmitted to the hospital. Slowly he began to improve.

We hunkered down all winter. Every day Gillian and I would take Cullen to kindergarten. The kindergarteners were learning their letters and Cullen decided to take Gillian to school for show and tell on G day. Cullen's friends at school began to call Gillian "G" and her nickname was born.

We were unable to have other children in our home that winter, for fear of infection and as a consequence Cullen and Gillian were each other's only playmates and they became incredibly close as we circled the wagons around our family.

It was mid-winter and I found myself headed to Mass one Sunday morning. My mood matched the weather-grey and dreary. I sat in the pew and waited for Mass to begin. In the quiet of the church my mind wandered... where had my wonderful life gone? Less than two years ago I had a perfect life and a healthy husband. The lector approached the pulpit and offered a welcome, it was pretty standard fare and varied little from week to week but something caught my attention as he indicated that today we were celebrating the Fifth Sunday in Ordinary Time. I shifted gears as my mind took me down another path.

The liturgical calendar marks the major events of the year, including: Advent, a season of preparation for Christmas; Christmas, the celebration of the birth of Christ; Lent, a season of preparation for Easter; the Easter Season, a celebration of the death and resurrection of Christ; and Pentecost, when the gift of the Holy Spirit was given. Most of the liturgical year, however, is referred to as Ordinary Time.

The word ordinary comes from the root word ordinal, which simply means, "numbered." And in fact the Sundays of Ordinary Time are indeed numbered. It was during Ordinary Time that Jesus did most of his teaching and performed most of his miracles.

I sat in the pew listening. The first reading was about the miseries of Job. Job was a good and faithful man who lost everything. The message I came away with was that even the just are made to suffer. This is something I knew all too well; but why? According to the pastor suffering is a test of fidelity. And then the Gospel according to Mark spoke about Jesus healing the sick and casting out demons. I was struck by the contrast.

I could fixate on the dark and the difficult. I did not want to be tested anymore. I was tired and weary. I understand Job. I get the suffering part. It is God I do not understand. In spite of being stripped of everything he held dear, Job remained faithful to God. In return for his faithfulness, God blessed Job with a new family and even greater wealth. Great. But I could not help but ask: what about Job's original children? Just when would God reverse the hand of fortune and restore my family? I did not want a new family; I wanted the one I had. Is that what this suffering was about, a test of faithfulness? There I was standing on the precipice, a strong wind or an unkind word and I could so easily fall from grace. I fear the fall. God help me.

So the question was, do I wait faithfully for God to change the course of my life? Or I could refocus my vision, keep the eyes of faith open, and look for the everyday miraculous.

I also thought about the other meaning of Ordinary Time: it is an undeniable fact that, for each of us, our days on this earth are numbered. So here I was in Church, and the spiritual message could not have been clearer: I was being asked to seek the miraculous in the ordinary and to wake up and recognize the extraordinary in this one precious life, as this life is short; don't waste it.

The question was, could I do it? I wasn't sure.

A couple of times a week I went by Fred's office to pick up boxes of files for him to review. He was still not out of the woods. He could not go to work as he could not be out associating with people for fear he would get an infection. Fred would lose his insurance if he did not work. Fred's boss allowed Fred to work from home. He was wonderful to Fred. Fred had worked for the prosecutor's office for 15 years and they took care of their own. As I walked out of Fred's office one day, with a box full of files for him to review, it occurred to me. This was an everyday miracle. I stopped mid-stride. It was true. Many people who are sick and out of work lose their income and fall into poverty. However, we retained our insurance and Fred retained his salary.

For the first time in many weeks, I felt a bit of relief from the inner burden I was carrying. We were indeed blessed. Okay, so this was an obvious miracle. If all the elements had aligned differently our fate could have been like Job's. Were there other miracles? If so, could I train myself to see them?

The Prosecutor's Office was getting a fair amount of national press as they were actively prosecuting Dr. Jack Kevorkian at this time. He was being tried for murder for assisting 130 people with physician-assisted suicide from 1990 to 1998.

Fred's boss, Richard Thompson, was publicly lambasted in the media as if he was on a personal witch-hunt to prosecute and persecute Dr. Kevorkian. It was difficult to watch the media's spin on this, as they painted Dick Thompson as cruel and unkind. We knew him differently. The decision he made to allow Fred to work at home saved us from financial ruin and allowed Fred to get the care he desperately needed to survive.

Fred struggled with his office's decision to prosecute Dr. Kevorkian. Dr. Kevorkian had said repeatedly, "Dying is not a crime." The people in Fred's office tiptoed around him when the topic would arise. Fred knew first hand what most people he worked with did not. He suffered. At this point in his life he endured the pain and suffering because his life was meaningful and he wanted it to continue. He was not ready to leave us and so he continued to subject himself to whatever was necessary to stay with us. But in the quiet of the night when we were alone he made me promise that come what might I would not prolong his suffering if and when he found it intolerable. I promised him that I would abide by his wishes, as difficult as this would be.

Over the course of the school year there were multiple outbreaks of chicken pox at St. Hugo's, the kids' school. If the kids contracted the chicken pox it could be fatal for Fred. A consequence of the BMT was that he no longer had immunity. The incubation period for the chicken pox is 21 days and the virus can be spread before the infected person shows any symptoms. Fred's doctor recommended that Fred move out of the house until we determined if the kids had been exposed. Every time another child came down with the chicken pox, we started over with the three-week window of opportunity for exposure and Fred's projected return home was pushed back again until he was out of the house for nearly 3 months.

Fred moved into the guest room at Shelley and Joel's. Their house was just down the street, two houses away from ours.

My girlfriends would call and joke with me about having conjugal visits with my husband. It might have been funny if your husband was well and home. I missed mine and after all we had been through, it was hard to know he was down the street and I still could not sleep with him, let alone have any real physical intimacy. I tried to put a good face on it. My friends did not mean any harm. However, they did not know how hurtful some of these cavalier comments were.

I was alone every night. The physical exhaustion of the day helped me fall asleep, but my worries invaded my dreams. All too often I would wake in the early morning, unable to fall back asleep. Yes, I knew that it was my turn to carry the load, but much was asked of me. I did the best that I could but there were times when it just did not seem good enough.

This journey belonged to Fred and I; unless someone else had walked this walk, they did not understand. How could they? I was 36 years old and Fred was 43. At this point in my life I did not know anyone who had walked this journey. I did not have a guide. I made it up as I went along.

I received so much unsolicited advice from friends and acquaintances, on how they would do things differently. Gram's wisdom came back to me, "*Save me from the well-intended. They mean well.*" They did not know what it was like to be on this path. I did not have time to engage in this. I let it go. I was having difficulty seeing anything miraculous in my everyday struggles but the clouds would part and soon what was hidden became clear.

I visited Fred when I could and brought meals for Shelley, Joel and Fred every night. I used the kids' little red wagon: Meals on Wheels. Fred needed nutritious food. And there was that laundry list of things he could not eat and things that he had to eat if he was to recover. So I cooked for them and delivered the meals and little by little his health and strength were returning.

One of the miracles was that the kids never got the chicken pox and the following year they were amongst the first in line to receive the new varicella vaccine.

Another miracle was that when Fred got sick he was blessed to have a sister and brother-in-law who loved him so much that they picked up their lives and moved down the street to be closer to him. They love one another and this chicken pox threat provided them an opportunity to spend this time together. This time spent together served to strengthen the bonds of their love for one another.

One evening we had some friends to our home for dinner. We were feeling grateful and uplifted as Fred was finally home and his health was improving. It had been a long hard fall and winter and we rejoiced in the coming of spring. After dinner, while we were still sitting at the table having tea, these well meaning friends decided this would be a good time to talk with Fred about whether he had accepted Jesus as his personal savior. They wanted to know if Fred had said the special prayer that would guarantee him a place in heaven.

In my heart of hearts I know they meant well. They approached this with only the best of intentions. Gram's wisdom came to me yet again, "*Save me from the well-intentioned. Just remember, they mean well.*" But I was so pissed off I could hardly see straight. Fred was obviously distressed by their implication that unless he uttered this magic spell that he would be damned to hell for all time.

I am uncertain how the evening ended, as my memories are clouded with the rage I felt at their audacity.

I would struggle with the events of this evening for a long time. I needed to find a way to forgive them so I could let this go. How could they have said these things to my beloved husband, given all that he had been through? I did not like the way I felt. In time my outrage and anger would dissipate. I came to see this as opportunity for learning as I confronted my own belief that there are many paths to God. I know that not everyone believes this to be true. Our dinner guests clearly believe that their path is the only path. I had long found this approach to salvation to be arrogant and self-righteous. Did these people truly believe that God loved them more than the rest of the human family? Did they really believe that Fred's soul would rot in hell for all time if he did not see the world through their very narrow lens? I could hardly wrap my head around this. But the truth of the matter was this: I needed to take a good long look in the mirror and acknowledge that if this path brought them closer to God then who was I to get in the way? The everyday miracle was this: when I confronted my own prejudices, against the fundamental Bible- banging Christians, I saw that I was not as open-minded and open-hearted as I proclaimed to be, or more importantly as I wanted to be. If I believe that the love of God for the human family is inclusive and not exclusive, and I do believe this, then that love is clearly extended to the Christian conservatives as well as to everyone else. When I acknowledged my own prejudices I was able to become more accepting to all those who seek a different way, even the Christian fundamentalists. This epiphany also started the healing of a long-standing riff that existed within my own family.

I had to work to see the miracles in the everyday. Fred's recovery was not without setbacks. We called it the dance of life, two steps forward and one step back. We were getting used to the pace of this and tried not to let the setbacks unravel us too much. Nonetheless, Fred seemed to be developing an uncanny ability to see things from a different, almost luminous perspective.

During one hospitalization, when Fred was in great agony, he wrote me this love letter:

Dear Jeanne,
As I sat here last night before I fell asleep, I began thinking of how much you mean to me. I guess it began midday when my thoughts went back to you dressed for our wedding. I remember you wondering if you could be fancier, lacier, more flowing or

whatever and all I could think of was how perfectly you were fashioned. As always, the most elegant balance of taste and fashion never detracting from your beautiful features.

I then moved on to you in the dark of my mind's eye, again this time the snapshot of you on our honeymoon in Greece standing in front of the ruins of the Agora. The main thing that kept coming to me was so ironic. The irony I'm referring to is that the beauty that mesmerized me then is only a portion and so different from the beauty that now takes my breath away. Quite honestly from the first time I saw you in tennis togs at Detroit Tennis and Squash, up through all of our courting stage, I was stunned by your physical beauty. Clearly I was very aware of the inner you and I'm sure that the inner radiance was probably the force that brought us together, but I ponder now over the changes that our/my love has taken. Over and over I can remember thinking you were the most beautiful woman I had ever seen. Your hair, body and facial features were so perfectly shaped. It's frightening to me now to find that the treasure that I cherish and love the most seems so different to me now.

Jeanne, I love you so much and I feel now for so many of the right reasons that it literally weakens me as I reflect on them. I am so blessed to share a life and a family with you. As I sit and reflect on "nothing happens by accident," I am further overwhelmed by the spiritual journey that we have taken to get to today. I'm sure that I omit much in my ignorance of what was happening but RCIA, Kirk's birth, change in health care, The Daily Word, the change from Dr. Magno to Dr Jana and Dr Siegel's book all come to mind as wonderful forms of Divine intervention.

Most of all honey, there's you. Your abiding faith in God has been a beacon that our family has been able to follow throughout my dis-ease, which it might properly be called. The change and love in my family was very notable thanks to your strength and courage.

I am extremely earnest when I say that there is no question in my mind that this has been harder on you. It's simply easier to be the one going through it rather than the spouse on the sidelines. By your example I feel that the kids have grown in ways too wonderful to exactly pinpoint. To witness Cullen's reliance on prayer and love of life gives me great sustenance and reason for my life. To see the joy in Gillian does the same.

I think I have mentioned this in the past but one of my greatest fears when I became ill was that a father's early death would cause bitterness in his children. I feared that they would be unable to see the goodness of life that has been the hallmark and special blessing of ours. I am forever hopeful that as all my fears dissolve into an even stronger faith of Divine order, our children's love of God has been unshakeably forged forever.

<u>Unseen Order</u>
– James Dillet Freeman

I can see the beauty
Where no beauty's there,
When all the trees are leafless
And all the fields are bare;
I can see the light
When the light is gone;
I can keep the faith at dark fall
As I did at dawn;
I can trust the tides returning
When it's still going out;
And keep on looking for the truth

161

Though mostly I find doubt.
There is an unseen order
I do not understand,
A higher wisdom and a love,
And I am in it's hand.

I read this poem this morning and I thought it was nice. Last night one of the nurses said that a friend quizzed her asking, "How can you believe in something that you cannot see?" I included the poem because of this question. I'm so thrilled with our children and the way you've raised them.

Well honey, I suppose it is only fitting that you had to wait seven years to get a love letter from me. It is a little maddening to realize that this is about the same time you spent with AH. Not to cheapen this note but rather as an admonition to me to go and love you up ASAP.

Thanks to you, fear and worry dissolve into a tremendous faith and focus in the <u>now</u>; let's keep up this focus for our benefit and the benefit of our family and friends.

Love always,
Fred

Most women never receive this kind of letter, but because of our life circumstances, I was the beneficiary of this beautiful testament to the way my beloved felt about me.

This was when it hit me. Human love is itself a miracle, given that we are capable of such incredible self-centeredness. And yet, at a time in his life when Fred could have been consumed with anger and self-pity, he was not. He was thinking of...me.

I have never felt so loved in my entire life. He knows me, with all my faults and human failings, and yet he loves me. The bond of love we had been forging grew even stronger.

Once Fred was out of the hospital, the challenges were far from over. For one thing, Fred could not return to the office because his immune system had been so severely compromised. He had not seen any of his colleagues since September—leaving him feeling isolated and home-bound.

For another thing, all of the drug treatments and radiation had greatly altered his appearance. One March afternoon when he was released from the hospital, Fred stopped by the Prosecutor's office. He could not go inside, so he walked around the side of the building, peered through a window on the first floor and waved to his former assistant. He wore a knit ski hat and his face was swollen from the steroids. Collette had worked for Fred for years and they were friends but she no longer recognized him and was frightened by this stranger who looked at her through the window.

When Fred told me about the incident, I knew this hurt his feelings and it broke my heart. And yet, I could see Fred's perspective on life changing and deepening. We talked about how life changes all of us; it is part of life, but it is the soul, the inner radiance that we need to look for. Fred is my beautiful, beautiful soul mate.

In the spring of 1994, Fred was back at home. He was feeling better but not well enough to return to work. He was still on a boatload of medications and would be for quite some time. I found myself having a difficult time finding the everyday miracles. If anything, I was caught up in all the little tensions and struggles of each day… and each night too.

The medications affected his sleep and his energy level. His sleep-wake cycle was a mess. Gillian was three and a half at the time, and an earlier riser. She was frequently up around 5 AM. Many mornings she would tiptoe into our bedroom to see if her Daddy was awake. I was torn between wanting him to sleep and wanting to let them share this time together. She regularly whispered in his ear to ask him to put on a movie for her and once it was started, she would send him back to bed. Her favorite movie was Disney's <u>Beauty and the Beast</u> and she had seen it hundreds of times but she always found the scene with the wolves to be very scary. Every time she watched the movie she came back into our bedroom to wake her Daddy. She would take him by the hand and lead him back to the family room. "Come on, Daddy, the wolves are coming." Morning after morning Fred would pick her up and sit her on his lap and they would watch the scary parts together. When she was no longer afraid she would tell him, "Thank you, Daddy, I'll be okay now, you can go back to bed."

I decided to let down my guard a bit. Something wonderful was happening here, and I didn't want either of them to miss it. And whatever it was I didn't want to miss it either.

As Fred's health improved he would take his little early riser out for a morning walk. He still needed to wear a surgical mask to protect himself from the possibility of infection. They dubbed these walks: Dog Walks. They would come back every morning in time for breakfast and Gillian would recount the number and types of dogs they had seen on their morning stroll. Her personal favorites were the 'doll nations.' There was something beautiful developing here, between the two of them, as Fred found a way to connect with his little girl.

One morning while Fred and Gillian were out for their walk, I found myself looking out the front window to see if I could spot them. There was Fred, savoring the sweetness of the moment. He was beaming down at Gilly, sheltering her, comforting her, building her up and feeding her spirit. The beauty of her childhood was not lost on him. As sick as he had been he could have been miserable, self-involved and draining. He would be entitled to be but he was not; instead he was a channel of unconditional love.

As I stood at the window watching them hold hands and walk down the sidewalk, I found myself savoring this moment too—because here again was the beauty of the miraculous in the everyday. As parents we love our children with a pure unselfish love and there is brilliance in that. Watching my beloved husband I see the love and presence of God take human form.

We did our best to find something to celebrate every day. One sunny morning while Fred was looking out the window into the garden he announced, "The Big Guy really out did himself today." I could not agree more. We had truly learned to appreciate the beauty of our lives and to be thankful for each and every day. We had come a long way since the dark days of the not-so-distant past.

But much as I loved the bright flashes of the miraculous, most of our days in Ordinary Time were like everybody else's–ordinary.

When the summer finally arrived Fred was doing so much better but the year had taken its toll on us. The summer found me taking care of my family, the house and now this extensive yard and garden. The kids wanted to be in the lake all day long, so I spent a good deal of the summer teaching swim lessons and playing lifeguard. Fred was not supposed to dig in the dirt as his doctors still considered his immune system to be compromised. I know him, it made him crazy when the gardens were not manicured, so I tried my best to keep up with the lawn and the gardens; otherwise I knew I would find him on his knees pulling weeds. By the time August rolled around I was ready to head out of town. I needed a vacation.

We took our summer vacation at the Jersey Shore where we would visit my sister, Susan and her family. At this point in our lives my sister and I were worlds apart. As we drove east, I realized that this might be a challenge. Although I have always considered Susan to be my dearest friend we had not been close through this crisis in my life. It was true; she was busy with her husband, and two small children of her own. But I had missed her and I was looking forward to this trip more than I can say. I needed a place where I could lay down my worries and rest my fears. I needed someone to help me carry my inner burdens.

This was our first trip away in almost a year. Susan was working in her antique shop in Cape May when we arrived. She knew that we were coming but even still, initially she did not recognize Fred. He had changed.

The more time one would spend with Fred, the easier it was to overlook the physical changes that had occurred and to focus instead on the essence of the man. Although his appearance had changed, the spirit of the man was not diminished by the trauma and tragedy of his illness, but rather was strengthened by his loving approach to his life's challenges. He was so strong and those who got to know him were awestruck by his strength, and his presence put others at ease.

Susan, Robert and their kids embraced us. Susan lovingly attended to every detail and I felt her love and compassion. We had a wonderful vacation. We caught crabs off their dock and to the fear and delight of the children the crabs escaped in the kitchen. The kids played from dawn to dusk at the beach and overall this vacation was a welcome escape from the long ordeal of the bone marrow transplant. I reconnected with my sister and she offered understanding and acknowledged the magnitude of the struggle we had been living. The opportunity to talk with her and to be listened to, validated my experience and allowed me to give up some of the load I had been carrying.

We are called to be Christ-like and to help lift the load for others. This week spent with my sister provided the time and space for an extraordinary renewal of our love for one another, a reconnection of our sisterhood. When it was time to return home it occurred to me that this was the next miracle hidden in my daily life. I felt strengthened and less alone as she helped me bear my load. This reconnection with Susan had been nothing short of an answer to a heartfelt prayer.

Something was happening to my eyesight—or rather to my vision. I was beginning to see the world differently. I could see and feel all of the difficulties. Of them there is no end. But once I began to see the extraordinary in our everyday life, this ordinary life took on a different quality.

Most often, this would happen in the most common experiences. That summer Cullen began to play soccer with his friends from school. Our little boy was a terrific little athlete. He had great hand-eye coordination and he was fast. He certainly did not take after his mother. Fred on the other hand was a great athlete. Fred played soccer in high school and he and Cullen would practice in the yard. Cullen spent hours taking shots on goal. He and his Dad would run up and down the hill in our side yard to increase their strength and endurance. These became known as– sweat races.

One afternoon while I was out weeding the garden and Cullen was running up and down the hill doing his sweat races he called out to me, "I can't wait 'til Dad gets home. I'm going to W-I-P-E his butt."

I started laughing as I told him what the word was that he just spelled. We both laughed so hard that we could hardly catch our breath when Cullen assured me that he has no intention of wiping anyone's butt; however he was not opposed to whipping his Dad's butt.

Gillian was in preschool and she spent the fall playing with the neighbor girls. They were a roving band of little girls and they played all sorts of imaginary games. One afternoon I overheard the girls negotiating the roles for the day's adventure.

Gillian said, "I'll be the Mom."

And Ellen replied, "Okay and I'll be the baby dinosaur." As if it was the most natural thing in the world for all mothers to have their own baby dinosaur.

Gillian and the three Hoxsie girls, who were our neighbors on the other side, spent weeks that fall trying to catch a kitten for Gillian. They used an old wash bucket and some grass and weeds for bait.

These children are my heart's delight. What I see in the children, and in all members of the human family, is the ability to transform the ordinary into the extraordinary. We need to see with our eyes open and seek out the beautiful and the delightful as it is always present. If only we take the time to look for it. There is something in the human spirit that has been created to do this. It is so obvious to little children. They marvel at the world but sometimes we lose our appreciation for the lives that we have been given as we get older.

What I began to see was this: our spiritual vision has to be cultivated. The ability to see the extraordinary, in the ordinary, needs to be recaptured and nurtured. It is valuable beyond wealth, because it gives us the ability to transform the dark into light.

CHAPTER 9

Everyday Struggles

Sometimes it was more difficult to see the miraculous than at other times.

In March 1994, Mary Kaye, Fred's Mom, began to fail. She was 64 years old and had type 1 diabetes since she was in her early thirties. She was hospitalized when she went into multi-organ system failure. She and Fred spoke on the phone, as Fred could not go visit her. It was not lost on Mary Kaye how critically ill she was. She had lived with chronic illness, and all of the repercussions, most of her adult life. Mary Kaye was Fred's role model for how to live, really live, with illness. Fred loved his mother and she him.

When Mary Kaye died that spring, Fred was sad but he was resolved. She did not let the important things of life remain unsaid. Perhaps that is what one learns when they live with illness because they are fully cognizant that their days indeed are numbered. They loved one another, their earthly relationship was complete and they knew that they would see one another again. Fred had no regrets about his relationship with his mother.

A couple days before she died, Mary Kaye was in the hospital and I spoke with her on the phone. I asked if there was anything I could do for her. She responded, "Please take care of Don."

How many times have the well-meaning and the well-intentioned said, "*Don't worry... God does not give you more than you can handle.*"

Really? I was barely holding on. It was the tail end of the long hard winter after the bone marrow transplant, Fred was quarantined down the street at his sister's, I have two kids who needed me, in the throes of all of this my mother-in-law died and now I was being asked to care for Don. God had really upped the ante.

Don was angry and unresolved about Mary Kaye's death. I don't think it ever crossed his mind that he might out live her. He did not like me, he never had. Mary Kaye's deathbed request would be hard for me to honor but I would try.

After Mary Kaye's death I went to their family home to help with some general housekeeping. They had a big five-bedroom house that had fallen into disrepair during Mary Kaye's illness and needed a good thorough cleaning. I spent the entire day cleaning the house from top to bottom and before I left I put on a pot of vegetable soup that I had made from scratch so Don would have something nutritious to eat.

When Fred called later to check in on his Dad he was told, "She is so slow. It took her all day to clean the house, and next time tell her to throw some meat in the soup." He was not exactly gushing over with gratitude but it was exactly the attitude I had come to anticipate from him.

The following fall Fred's Dad was hospitalized with emphysema. He was a chain smoker and smoked nearly 3 packs of cigarettes everyday for the better part of 50 years. When he was released from the hospital he was still much too weak to go home alone, so he spent a few months recuperating at Shelley and Joel's house, just down the street from us. Fred had moved out of their guest room and Don moved in. Once again, Shelley and Joel opened their home and opened their hearts.

We all had dinner together about once a week. One evening Cullen was practicing his piano on an electronic keyboard. He flipped on some pre-programmed selection complete with a full orchestra. Don was listening from the other room and commented to Fred. "I think Cullen really has some talent." Here was a moment of shared laughter and joy and peace in an otherwise stormy relationship.

Don argued with Fred about everything. Fred could not make a comment about the Detroit Tigers without Don turning the conversation around; so before you knew it Don was raving on about Tom Monahan, the owner of the Tigers and his support of Catholic charities, which somehow led to an unbridled recounting of Don's distain for the Catholic Church and Fred's membership in it. Don was angry about the death of his wife and he took it out on Fred.

Don had been a successful, prominent attorney who had spent his life accumulating power, wealth and possessions. He was also an alcoholic and due to his drinking he had lost most of what he valued and he was angry. Fred had consciously made very different choices than his father and Don resented it. Although also an attorney, Fred had chosen a different path from his father and Don did not approve.

People often release their anger on the people they know are safe, people who will love them unconditionally. Fred forgave his father's transgressions over and over again. However, just because he forgave him did not mean that his father's words did not hurt him. We talked about this and I think it helped. Fred tried to let go and not focus on his father's negativity, but rather he tried to understand him and love him where he was.

I began to see that sometimes life's miracles are not just handed to us, not just simply revealed when we are ready to see, but instead they require work. I decided to try and apply grace to Don. What is grace? But an unmerited kindness or favor. This would be a challenge for me, as Don clearly did not like me. This would require work.

I was left to wonder: what could I do to get through to this difficult, difficult man...

One day before Thanksgiving Shelley asked me to put a turkey in the oven at her house. She was working and was planning to have a turkey dinner as she and Joel wanted to have an early Thanksgiving because they would be out of town on Thanksgiving Day. When I went to their house I found that Don was in the garage having a cigarette and the oxygen tubing was under the door and oxygen was running. He looked at me as if I had caught him with his hand in the cookie jar. Shelley and Joel had made only one stipulation when they brought him home with them and that was that he would not smoke in their house. Here he was smoking and with the oxygen on. He could have blown himself up as well as burnt the whole house down. He begged me not to tell. I was in a difficult position, holding the secret of a man who did not like me to begin with.

I expressed my concern for his safety and then decided to keep his confidence.

Don and I never spoke of this again.

But as time passed, and my view of life shifted, a miracle born of this tough relationship would be revealed. I came to realize that it is one thing to be looking for grace for yourself. It is another to be asked to be grace for someone else....especially for difficult people. Is this not what Jesus asks of us? We are asked to love one another, to treat others the way that we want to be treated and to love our enemies. It is not difficult to love and be kind to those who love you, that is the easy part. In contrast, loving those who do not love you or even like you, that's tough.

But the next summer, Don would buy airline tickets for the whole extended family to travel to Yosemite National Park in California for the wedding of Mary Kaye's niece. This was an incredible act of generosity and love that I had not seen from him before. Everyone had a wonderful time. It was a time of good health for both Fred and Don and a time of love and healing.

Two months later, Don would die of emphysema. Fred had a difficult time coming to terms with his father's passing as during so much of their lives they were at odds with one another. Don's life had been full of regret. He suffered from depression and he brought his negativity to those he encountered. I do not know what he was thinking or feeling as he drew close to the end of his life, as we did not have that kind of relationship. I believe that, perhaps, there was at least one small miracle. Somewhere in the midst of Don's angry isolation, for just a few moments, I connected with this man and was able to show him grace. I reflect on our trip to Yosemite, I believe that Don truly appreciated the beauty of northern California and the love of his family. He was able to experience the joy of being generous in his ability to make the trip possible for all of us. I pray for his soul and that in the next life he will be blessed by the grace of God.

There would be other opportunities for the extraordinary to be manifested in spite of the struggles of our ordinary lives.

In the winter of 1996, Fred and I, Shelley and Joel, and Kirk and his girlfriend Janine worked together to close their parent's estate. There needed to be a sale as Fred's mother was an antique dealer and she and Don had acquired a houseful of antiques and personal property that needed to be disposed of.

Fred and each of his siblings took turns choosing items that they would prefer to keep rather than sell. We did this every weekend, all weekend for months. It was a time of bonding and childhood remembrances for Fred, Shelley, and Kirk. We worked and shared meals and plenty of laughter.

This was a healing time for them as they came to terms with the loss of both of their parents.

Fred's family situation made me think of my re-bonding experience with my own sister as well as my estranged relationship with my brother. Most of the time it is not the strangers in our lives that cause us the most pain, it is the people we love and trust the most who are capable of wounding us most deeply with unkind words, or more likely, indifference. Those we love the most are able to hurt us because they know intimately where our weaknesses and sensitivities lie. On the other hand, as I saw with Fred's siblings, we can also be part of one another's healing for the very same reasons; it is a choice we make.

I did not know it then, but I would need this added ability, not just to recognize, but also to find the miracle in the darkness...because things were about to change again for Fred and I.

When Fred went back to work fulltime, there were still concerns for his vulnerability to infection, so his supervisor altered his job responsibilities. Prior to getting sick, Fred was a trial attorney for the Prosecutor's office in the Circuit Court. In the courtroom he had daily contact with a large number of people. In his new job, Fred was the Chief Assistant in the Circuit Court. He worked with the young attorneys developing trial strategies. Everyone in the office knew that they should only approach Fred in person if they were well. The line of his colleagues would form outside of his office door on a daily basis, which began to be known as the Fred Line.

The subsequent years were punctuated with episodes of general well-being and episodes of unexpected illness.

Fred was hospitalized periodically with pneumonia and high fevers of undetermined origins that required immediate action and IV antibiotics.

These exacerbations and relapses would easily put me on edge again. Frequently the remedy was an extensive course of steroids and all the accompanying side effects.

For one thing, Fred was always hungry when he was on steroids and to quote him, he felt like he could "eat the doors off the refrigerator." When on steroids his weight would fluctuate from his usual 160 lbs to 195 lbs. Most of the weight was because the medication caused the fluid to accumulate in his face, the back of his neck and in his abdomen.

More difficult for us all was that Fred's personality changed when he was on steroids. Fred who was a calm and gentle soul could become irritable and short-tempered with minimal aggravation.

One evening I had gone out with my girlfriends and Fred was getting the kids bathed and off to bed. Cullen had been messing around and generally irritating Gillian and Fred had just about enough. He was tired and wanted to get the kids in bed. By Fred's own report, he had grabbed Cullen by the arm, swatted him on the butt with his hand and yelled at him. Cullen had rarely seen his Dad lose his temper as he yelled back at him, "You're the worst father in the world! You're worse than Pappy!" It was at a time when Fred was reading <u>The Adventures of Huckleberry Finn</u> to Cullen and Pappy was Huck Finn's abusive drunken father. Gillian started to cry as she was not used to this kind of yelling and then Cullen and Fred cried too.

It was not difficult for us to forgive him, as I explained to the children that it was the drugs that made him behave this way and becoming short-tempered was beyond his control. It was much more difficult for Fred as he knew he was not himself and this messed with his sense of inner peace. Fred and the kids began to refer to his steroid irritability as "feeling like Pappy."

And so we entered a new era—of the steroid roller coaster. They always started Fred out on a massive dose of steroids but it would take several months to wean him off the drugs, as stopping the steroids too quickly can send a person into an adrenal crisis.

And just when we thought we were out of the woods, Fred developed an obscure complication from the bone marrow transplant that caused his skin to be bruised from the chest down. When the doctor put him back on steroids to treat this again, I cried. This bruising was a sign of graft vs. host disease. Graft vs. Host is where the transplanted cells from Kirk's bone marrow (the graft) attacked Fred's body (the host). Some GVH is a good thing as it is an immune response and can recognize malignant cells as foreign and help remove them, but when the reaction is too severe it puts the host, Fred, in mortal danger.

Fred had only been off the steroids for a few months and now he was back on them again. The high doses that were required initially kept Fred from sleeping. His sleep-wake cycle was a mess. I don't know how he could function on so little sleep for months and months on end but somehow he managed.

One morning I woke up and Fred was not in bed. I found him in the kitchen. He was quite proud of himself, for when he could not sleep he decided to rearrange the kitchen for me and he had taken all the things that HE thought I didn't use and put them in the attic. I kept my mouth shut as I climbed two sets of stairs to get to the attic to retrieve my angel food cake pan and a whole variety of other "unnecessary" kitchen utensils.

As the months on steroids took their toll, I would have to work to find the silver lining to this dark cloud, to find the miraculous in this struggle. The path was getting steeper. And then, there it was. One night when he could not sleep Fred decided to write Valentine's Day letters to all of our friends. By the time I was up and before I had even had my breakfast, the letters had been stamped and were in the mail. I must admit that I was worried, what had he written under the influence of these crazy drugs?

It did not take me long for me to find out how much our friends loved their letters. Each letter was personalized and written from his heart. Fred had expressed his love and gratitude for their individual contribution to his recovery.

In this journey, I have looked for the answers to my prayers. I have looked for signs of healing as I prayed for Fred's illness to vanish. I prayed for love, understanding and support as I struggled to keep my faith and my family together body and soul. In short, I wanted the world to be transformed according to my vision for health, happiness and peace. But right in front of me was a miracle of another kind.

In the midst of his pain and suffering, the deeper, richer aspects of Fred's spirit had begun to shine—and not just shine, but blaze like a beacon. Fred was learning some kind of lesson. While I kept seeking the answers to prayer in the physical world and looking for outer changes...yet in the quiet of the day I began to realize that the spirit could also grow and change...the spirit could manifest the miracles of health, happiness and peace, and if we do not look for these we can miss them.

For the moment I had to be fixed in the here and now. The kids were in school and beginning to go through their own challenges. Gillian had started first grade and she was one of the youngest in her class. I had debated having her repeat kindergarten and having her wait to start first grade until she was a year older. The school counselor made me feel like a crazy woman when she told me, "It would be criminal to hold her back. Besides we have a special reading program to help bring the younger students up to speed." So against my better judgment I consented to have her start.

I was stressed, I suffered and I could not sleep for every day my beautiful little girl was beaten down by first grade. Gillian knew her letters but she would rather play than learn to read, and all the encouragement in the world did not make her ready to read when she simply was not ready.

One winter evening while I was preparing dinner, Gillian and Cullen were sitting at the kitchen counter.

"Raise your hand if you like yourself," Gillian commanded in her best teacher voice.

Cullen and I looked at one another and we both raised our hands, but Gillian did not.

"Raise your hand if you love yourself," Gillian commanded again.

Again Cullen and I raised our hands but Gilly did not. I stopped what I was doing and turned to my little blonde six-year-old. She had tears in her eyes and her lips started to quiver. Her little face showed her pain and the utmost despair.

"Honey, why don't you love yourself?" I asked as gently as I could. Cullen looked at his little sister with love and concern.

"How can you love yourself when you are not a good reader?" Gillian buried her head on my shoulder and started to sob. The trauma of the last few months were released and the floodgates were opened. She began to cry so hard that she could not catch her breath.

Cullen gently kissed his sister on the top of her head. "I love you G." He quietly left the kitchen for at 8 years old he knew she needed her Mommy and some privacy. The sadness he felt for her was written on his face.

She sobbed uncontrollably about how mean her reading teacher, Sister Mary Lynn, was to her. The stories poured forth. Gilly had been strong and brave for months but this teacher was mean-spirited. Enough was enough and I was pissed. I told Gillian that her Daddy and I would not let this continue.

That night after the children were in bed, Fred and I discussed our options yet again. Fred spoke of the wisdom of the garden. "I have learned a great deal from my years in the garden. Some flowers bloom in the spring and some flowers bloom in the fall. Flowers need sunshine, water and the right kind of soil and with the patient, loving hand of the gardener they will bloom when they are meant to." Our children are our flowers. Gilly needed love and patience to bloom as she was meant to, not this heavy-handed approach. Fred began to refer to the reading program at St. Hugo's as "The Vince Lombardi School of Reading," as in "...we have ways of making you read," and her teacher became known as Sister Mary Pit Bull.

The next morning Cullen and Gilly went to school and I went to the principal's office. I had a good relationship with Sister Margaret and she sat and listened to my concerns. I told her that I wanted Gillian to return to kindergarten and that I wanted her to start first grade again next fall. She called Gillian into her office and asked her what she thought about returning to kindergarten. Her little face lit up and she asked sweetly, "Could I?"

In that moment the decision was made.

When I told Fred what happened at Gillian's school, he beamed. Again, there was that clear light within him. Fred was clear thinking, patient, loving and kind. He had a deeply developed sense of compassion. His wisdom was not bound by social convention. More and more his decisions were made in accordance with the laws of the natural world and with little concern for the judgments of others. He was an extraordinary man living in an ordinary time; he truly was a beacon of light.

CHAPTER 10

Mystery Trips

I did my best to keep looking for small miracles amidst some pretty difficult and painful days. But occasionally, life would deliver us a wonderful respite. Fred would be feeling well and we would shift our focus and it would be easy to find the good as it was all right in front me, like sweet low hanging fruit, ripe and ready for the taking.

Before the illness, Fred and I had been on an all out quest to see the world. But now so much had changed and we learned to modify our lust for high adventure and travel by planning things at the spur of the moment in something our family learned to revere as "mystery trips." We did this when Fred was feeling well and we knew we needed to capitalize on the moment.

I would secretly pack the suitcases and put them in the trunk of the car while the kids were sleeping or otherwise occupied. We would get in the car under the pretense of going to see Grandma, the grocery store or a movie and we would be off on a family adventure. It wasn't until we had passed the turn off to said destination that the kids began to ask questions.

"You missed the turn to Grandma's." Cullen would say as he was very observant and astute with directions. When we did not immediately turn the car around or acknowledge that a mistake had been made, he knew something was up.

"We're not going to Grandma's, are we?" When his question was met with a smile rather than an answer he was incredulous. "You said we were going to Grandma's. Where are you taking us?"

"To the monkey house," Fred responded as he kept driving, "we are going to put the two of you in the monkey house with all the other little monkeys."

"Daddy, I like monkeys," Gilly piped up from the back seat.

"Gilly, they're not taking us to a monkey house," Cully told her, as he was the older brother and thus the voice of authority. "Come on Dad, I want to know. This isn't fair; you said we were going to Grandma and Grandpa's. I bet Grandpa's waiting to play tennis with me."

Cullen started to get frustrated, "Mom, make him tell. Gilly wants to know too. Right, Gilly?"

"Mommy, you can tell us." Gilly added in sweetly.

I pulled the atlas from a satchel by my feet and handed it to the kids in the back seat. "See if you can figure it out."

After the first time when they received inadequate explanations to their reasonable questions, they began to understand what was transpiring. There would be shouts of glee, "Are we going on a mystery trip?"

The standard response would be, "If we told you, it wouldn't be a mystery."

This usually evolved into a game of twenty questions complete with only yes or no answers. In the process the kids learned how to read maps, learn about geography but mostly we just had fun.

Some of our mystery trips took us to Florida, to Niagara Falls, the Pictured Rocks in the Upper Peninsula, amusement parks, Mammoth Cave, the Smokey Mountains, the Jersey Shore, New York City and camping trips.

Even though Fred was better, "better" was a relative term. There was still so much potential danger. I met a side of myself that I hadn't really known before...the voice that asked all of the "what if questions." This part of me saw all the risks and all the dangers, and I did not know this woman and I did not like her very much either, and I certainly did not want to hear her nagging worries and her fears.

The reality was that Fred could get sick when we were far from home and far from the doctors who cared for him on an ongoing basis. We always needed to be relatively close to a major medical center so departures for out of the way, remote, third world adventure travel was not a good idea. Still, Fred liked to be wildly free himself. We wanted our kids to fall in love with life and to explore the world. I decided that my head could be full of what ifs...? But I consciously tried to let the worry go. How could I hold back?

During February in the winter 1994, we headed up to my parents' vacation home at Sugar Loaf in Cedar, Michigan. We spent a week skiing. The kids went to ski school in the morning and we would ski as a family in the afternoon. At the end of the week Gillian, who was 4 years old, pulled me aside to tell me about her 22-year-old ski instructor, "Mom, I think I love him."

She left me and went to give him a big hug and to thank him for helping her learn to ski. He smiled at her and he looked like he had never seen such a little cutie in his life. He gave me a smile and said, "She's great." He would be the first of many to capture her heart and fall for her endearing ways.

One afternoon Fred and Cullen were skiing together and I was skiing with Gillian. She and I took the chairlift up the face of the most difficult hill at the resort. It was appropriately called Awful-Awful. I watched as my six-year-old made his way across the moguls and my husband was rolling down the hill, ass over apple cart. It looked like a yard sale. He sat up and started to laugh. He was not hurt. I hesitated. I wanted to admonish them both for being so brazenly careless. What in the name of heaven were they doing on this hill?

Suddenly, a familiar feeling came rushing back. Fear. Fear of injury. Fear of loss.

Instead I held my tongue and let them go. I said to Gillian, "I cannot watch them. They both make me crazy. Let's go ski the backside."

"You're right, Mommy, they're crazy. Let's ski Devil's Elbow," and she led the way.

In June 1994, Fred was well. Fred's dad had gifted us with airline tickets so we could attend a family wedding in Yosemite. Fred and I and the kids extended the trip for three weeks and traveled throughout Northern California. We spent Father's Day hiking to Bumpus Hell at the Lassen Volcanic Park and ended the day around the campfire. Fred told us that he was the happiest man alive. Peace and joy covered us like a blanket and provided us protection from all the influences beyond our control.

At least at this moment, that was the way it felt.

There was one mystery trip that was not to be... when Gillian's fifth birthday arrived in August I asked her where she would like to have her birthday party. I was expecting her to suggest a party in the back yard or by the lake, perhaps the bowling alley or water park. She paused momentarily and casually suggested that she would like to go to Greece for her birthday, as she had never been to Greece on her birthday. I guess I did not need to worry about being able to implant a love of travel and exploring the world in this little one.

As it turned out, Fred was hospitalized on G's birthday with a blood clot in his leg. They did some testing and determined that the clot was not stable and only hanging by a thread. The doctors decided they needed to do an emergency procedure to thread a Greenfield filter into the vena cava for they feared the clot would release and go either to his lungs or to his brain. In either case, given the size of the clot, it could be fatal.

I waited with Fred, as they prepared the operating room. I was sick with fear. As I stood beside him and held his hand, he tried to lighten the moment, "Don't worry honey, they are just going to slip a little titanium cocktail umbrella in the blood vessel to catch that clot and I'll be good to go."

I smiled as leaned over to kiss him and I feared this might be our last good-bye. "I love you so."

"And I love you." He responded. The tears rolled down my cheeks and as they rolled him into the operating room, he blew me a kiss and winked.

I sat in the surgical waiting room, silent, dark and alone again. The minutes ticked by dreadfully slow as I waited. I tried to be still and just be with God as I waited for the surgeon to come through the door. And then there he was. He held my hands and nodded. I knew what this meant as his face said it all: another disaster averted. The procedure was successful.

Later that night as I made the midnight drive home from the hospital I thought: life had granted me so many blessings both miraculous and mysterious. Yet hidden within all the moments of freedom and joy was a basic fact of life that I did not want to deal with, the other meaning of Ordinary Time.

As I made my way down the miles and miles of interstate my mind had plenty of time to wander. And wander it did on this summer night as I contemplated the message from Ash Wednesday. Every year in the dead of winter, the Church called us to remember that we are mortal and our days are numbered. As the ashes from last year's burnt palms are rubbed on the foreheads, the priest would say, "*Remember man that thou art dust and unto dust thou shall return."* (Genesis 3:16) I did not want to think about this. Yet tonight my husband had been spared again and I was haunted by the reality that death had again crept close to Fred and again he was spared. How many times had he been spared and how many more times would he cheat the hand of death? I did not want to ask this question, for fear loomed with gratitude that night.

All of our lives hang so precariously by a thread. We are always just one heart beat and one breath away from the end of this world. Fred and I have been on a mystery trip…into all those mysteries of life in the face of death that no one wants to explore. I could hang my head and wring my hands at the terrible hardships we have had to endure.

On that drive home I realized that something inside me had shifted and changed. I no longer saw life's difficulties as merely "inconvenient" or even "terrible." We had been afforded the opportunity to really look at how fragile our hold on this life was and thus the blessings of our lives were not taken for granted.

All around our mystery trips and Fred's reoccurring bouts with disease, life was just about as normal for us as it was for any other family with growing kids.

When Cullen was in second grade he got into trouble at school. One of his little friends was caught skipping down the hallway singing a little melody, "Mrs. So&So's husband is a fucking idiot," was the refrain.

When the assistant principal, Sister Mary Ellen, who the children lovingly referred to as Sister Hairy Melon, pulled him aside, she asked little Jonathon to repeat himself. And he did. Her follow up question to this little second grader was, "Where did you hear that?"

To which Jonathon promptly replied, "Cullen Miller told me so."

Cullen and Jonathon were called into the assistant principal's office, along with their mothers. I felt like I was being punished because my child said a bad word and something mean. This reflected poorly on me and on my family. I was upset. I felt like a bad parent.

That night when Fred came home from work I followed him into the bedroom. He sat on the bed as he took off his shoes. When I began to tell him the story, he rolled back on the bed and was laughing his head off. He was laughing so hard that he could hardly speak.

"I can't believe you are laughing. I don't think this is funny." I was still remembering the shame I felt when I sat with this stern nun, as she admonished the children. And now my husband was splitting his gut with laughter.

He could hardly get the words out when he sputtered, "Well, is it true?"

I looked at him as if he had lost his mind. "Is what true?"

"Is the guy a fucking idiot . . . You know the truth is a defense." Fred was still laughing.

"Oh great, I see our little apple hasn't fallen far from your tree." In this moment I lightened up and began to see the humor. My reaction was way over the top. Fred helped me see that this was not the end of the world and that I needed to gain some perspective. However funny he found this, when he talked to Cullen he treated the incident as if it was a major offense and stressed that

Cullen needed to be careful how he used his words because words can hurt people.

In the years that followed, I grew to know and love Sister Mary Ellen. She helped my children and all the children of the school learn many things by her steadfast loving presence. She set high expectations for the children and they did not want to disappoint her and so they stretched and grew under her tutelage.

In the spring Fred and I were invited to go to Hilton Head for a week with Fred's boss, Ron and his wife, Margaret.

We had difficulty getting someone to watch the kids and it looked like we were going to have to turn down this generous invitation. In the eleventh hour, our dear friends Denis and Jill Naeger offered to watch the kids so we could get away. I cannot begin to find the words to express my gratitude for this generous gift. There are people in our lives who always seemed to know what it was that we needed, and in spite of the personal sacrifice that was entailed, they found a way to help. In doing so they made our lives better, richer and more complete. In a few words, Jill is this friend to me. Time and time again she has come through for me.

Our kids had a wonderful time. Gillian went with Jill everyday to pick up their four boys at school. They attended Our Lady of Refuge but Gillian dubbed the school "Our Lady of Red Shoes." Jill has all boys and she loved having a little girl in her house and little Gillian blossomed with Jill's attention. It is a love affair that would endure for years.

The boys teased Gillian and she relished it and learned a few things, too. She learned to make bunny ears over someone's head when photographs were being taken. When she was spotted, she would climb on to the person's lap and say, "Kiss me now and marry me later." We howled with laughter the first time she did this, only to find out that Jill's boys taught her this. Delightful childish antics.

When Jill asked Cullen to toss the salad for dinner he asked, "Where?" That's my boy always going for the laugh even as a little kid. They found him entertaining and precocious.

Fred was feeling well when we were in Hilton Head and we were optimistic about our future. We played golf, tennis and rode bikes. And in the evenings he would wine and dine me. We decided to buy a timeshare to celebrate our tenth wedding anniversary. We needed some time together. We celebrated where we had been, our lives together and our love for one another.

The day school was out we decided to go on another mystery trip, a camping trip to The Pinery Provincial Park on Lake Huron with four other families from St Hugo's. This would become an annual tradition and all the kids who participated would grow to count it among their favorite childhood memories. We camped, played in the sand dunes, shared meals and campfires. It was a new experience for some of the families. Some of the parents took to camping better than others. The camping trips became legendary amongst the children and every year more and more families joined us.

We all learned a great deal from the situation we found ourselves in such as:

Life is full of surprises.

Be flexible enough to move to Plan B at a moment's notice.

Be open to all that life brings you.

Enjoy the adventure.

Be present in your own life. Now. You will not get this moment back.

Make the best of the situation you find yourself in.

Do not wish things to be different, for if you do, you will miss this beautiful moment.

Live life awake. Embrace it in its entirety.

We all have things to learn. If we miss the lesson, we will need to learn it again and again.

Most of all, allow yourself to embrace life and all its mysteries. This journey of life is the greatest mystery trip of all.

CHAPTER 11

Extraordinary Time

When Gillian started first grade I had an opportunity to return to work. I had been on a ten-year hiatus from the world of paid employment when I was offered the position of Director of Health Education at Detroit Country Day School. This was not the type of work I had done before. I had never been in the classroom, except as a student; how difficult could teaching be? The schedule worked well with my family. I could work while my children were in school, I would be home in the evenings, and I would have my weekends and summers free. This could be the ideal job for this time in my life. I viewed this job as a Godsend and I decided to accept it with the expectation that I would work there for a year or two while the kids were little.

I was 39 years old at the time, and I was operating under the assumption that life had thrown me some fairly considerable challenges. All things considered, I felt that I had risen to the challenges fairly well. I was the first to acknowledge that I still had so much to learn, but my first year of teaching, high school juniors as a health teacher a.k.a. sex education teacher, challenged me in ways I had never conceived of. I felt as if I had been broad-sided by a bus, and I never saw it coming.

Detroit Country Day is an exclusive private school. It is a multicultural school where the children of privilege attend. These students are such bright lights and are the future leaders of our country and our world, but now they are still teenagers and thus in the need of guides, mentors and people to love, lead and listen to them.

During my first year, however, I was a 39-year old novice and these kids had a great deal of fun at my expense.

I was teaching sex ed to a group of students who thought they were all knowing about all things. Their collective attitude reeked of intellectual arrogance, "What could this middle-aged woman possibly teach me?"

Early on, I laid down some ground rules. I told the students that they could ask me any question they wanted to, but they could not use street language. They must speak in a way that is respectful to themselves, to me, and to the subject matter. I feared some of the students might be shy or embarrassed, as I might have been decades ago. One day I had them submit their questions into a bowl, so they would be anonymous.

I pulled the questions one at a time from the bowl. I read them aloud and then I attempted to answer the questions. Bad idea. Oh, this must rank right up there with the world's worst ideas in the field of teaching.

The questions were outrageous. One was worse than the next. Clearly the only person who was embarrassed was me. But, I was laughing so hard, at the insolence of these kids that I could hardly read the questions aloud, let alone answer them.

I have blocked most of them from my memory, as a way to protect myself from the pain and humiliation of it all. But I do recall a few of the questions, for example, "What is an aphrodisiac?" When I read the question aloud, one of my students, Ryan, who was about 5'8" tall and 260 pounds, sporting a blonde buzz cut, jumped up on top of the desk and began to gyrate his pelvis, announcing to the previously uninformed that he was in fact an aphrodisiac. The class deteriorated into peals of laughter.

I pulled out another question from the bowl. Written on the folded slip of paper was the question, "What does semen taste like?" The lesson for the day was scrapped.

One afternoon the Director of the school, my boss, Brad, stopped by my classroom unannounced to observe me, the new teacher. I later learned that this was a fairly routine practice but I did not know that at the time. At the end of my lecture, on testicular cancer, I offered to answer any questions that the students might have. One of my students asked, "Is it safe to use Saran Wrap when performing oral sex on a woman? Will Saran Wrap prevent the transmission of bacteria and viruses and other infectious organisms?"

Another asked, "Are edible condoms safe? What flavors do they make?" I wanted to crawl under the door and go directly to my car and never return again. The thought crossed my mind, perhaps they could mail me my purse and I would never have to see any of these people again. Instead I muddled through the questions and tried to retain my composure in the presence of my boss and these Teenage Creatures from the Black Lagoon. Dear God, how did I ever get myself into this?

The next day, I got a call from Brad's secretary. He wanted to meet with me in his office at 11 AM. It was my free period. I was certain I would be chastised and probably fired. Instead he told me that I handled the students and their questions pretty well. He thought it was a good thing that the students were comfortable enough with me to ask the questions that they really needed the answers to. I guess I'm a better actress than I thought, because underneath it all I was absolutely rattled.

So, I persevered out of sheer stubbornness. I never really have felt the need to be the conquering champion but I am much less comfortable being an abject loser. The fact of the matter is that I do not like to fail.

Fred supported me in this new career venture. We laughed. I struggled. I grew. I figured it out. I made two friends at school, that first year, who were veteran teachers. Their support was immeasurably helpful to me. Arlene Rama and Nora Labiano led with their hearts and they extended their love and kind ways to their students and also to me. I stretched and grew into my new career with their guidance.

My friends found it hilarious that I was a sex ed teacher. My job became the frequent topic of cocktail party conversation and I was easily cast as the butt of the joke. Repeatedly I was asked if there was a lab for my class. I learned to laugh at myself and with my students, and in doing so, my confidence and competence grew to the point where I absolutely loved my job.

On the surface, things were looking good. Fred continued to work for the Prosecutor's Office as the Chief Assistant Prosecutor of the Circuit Court. They were good to him and he was happy in his job too.

Fred was in remission. Yet he still battled the ramifications of the bone marrow transplant. The total body irradiation had left him with a frozen shoulder and they were talking about doing a total shoulder replacement. We discussed the pros and cons of the surgery and decided to put the operation on hold for a while. He joked that it had impacted his tennis serve but he would just have to live with an underhand serve until Cullen started beating him. Another ramification of the radiation was that Fred had developed cataracts in both eyes. He had the clouded lenses removed and new lenses implanted. This is a fairly common malady in older people but generally unheard of for someone in their forties.

One night after the kids were in bed and we had a quiet moment to talk, Fred confided to me, "My life is good. I feel a little like a three-legged dog. I'm not the same as I once was but I'm just happy to be here." We continued to learn from this rough journey. There had been so many hospitalizations and readmissions, fevers, adverse reactions to medications, pain, broken bones, blood transfusions, antibiotics, wheelchairs, more chemo and more steroids. More than ten times, Fred's doctors had confided to me that they did not think that Fred would survive this time and more than ten times they had been wrong.

One summer evening, I watched Fred from the deck. He had worked all day but in the evening he sat in the Adirondack chair providing a running commentary on the kids' dives as they performed various jumps, dives and cannonballs off the dock into the lake. I was struck by his extraordinary goodness and the joy he radiated in this moment. What was it that kept him going? He never complained and God knows he had ample reason to. His physical beauty had been stripped away, and yet the essence of the man, his soul, radiated in the debilitated shell of his very human form. I loved him more and more with each passing day. I thought I knew what love was as I had been blessed to have known love all of my life. This journey had taught me to love differently and more completely.

Our children watched and observed. When they are older they will tell me that they thought all marriages were like ours. As adults they would learn differently, but they had seen what real love looks like.

Freddy is my soul mate, and our bond to one another is eternal.

Our day-to-day life was good and we were happy. But on another level the ground was starting to shift again. Did Fred know I needed preparation, too?

Fred threw me a surprise 40th birthday party at Shelley and Joel's house in the spring of 1997. He sent out invitations to all of our friends with my high school graduation picture on it. The party was planned for a week before my birthday and I was totally taken by surprise. Friends from many different parts of my life attended the party. Friends from childhood, friends from college, friends from different places I had worked, and from our neighborhood. Fred did a great job putting the guest list together. It was comprehensive and inclusive. I felt loved. To top it off he had commissioned a birthday cake that was a total work of art. On the cake Cleopatra was being carried by her man slaves and the writing said, "*Happy 40th Birthday...to the Queen of De-Nile.*"

Truer words were never spoken. I have reflected on Fred's insight into me over the years. It very well may have been denial but it worked for me. And I think it worked for my family. I was coping. I tried my best to create positivity in the midst of doom and gloom...to keep us all on an even-keel, and to live as normal as possible, given that we were always living in the shadow of death.

Fred teased me. He openly told others I was in denial...but I could see that focusing on the light and the good in life was helping Cullen and Gillian grow up to be normal, happy and just plain zany kids.

Cullen had always done well in school and schoolwork came easily for him. However, when he was bored, which happens frequently to very bright children, he would act out. When he was in third grade he tormented his poor teacher with his antics. Whenever she turned her back to write on the board he climbed onto his desktop and danced, much to the delight of his classmates. They would giggle and laugh, and before the teacher could turn around to see why the class was laughing, Cullen would be back in his seat taking notes. This went on for months until the day he tipped the desk over and fell off the desk onto the floor with a crash.

One day this same teacher caught him talking with one of his pals on the way back from Mass. She was furious with him. My guess is that there had been multiple offenses but this was the one she chose to focus on. She had him write me a letter explaining his latest transgression, and she required that he bring it home for my signature. I never saw the letter because Cullen handled the situation himself and forged my signature, pretty well I might add, but in error he signed the letter– *Love, Jeanne.* Now he was in deep trouble for third grade forgery. The angrier this teacher became with her students, the more the kids tried to find a way to jerk her chain and jerk they did.

Cullen is a very likable person. He has always had lots of friends. He was the class clown and the Pied Piper. He still is. If Cullen is doing something, everyone else wants to do it too.

As parents, Fred and I learned to trust our gut instinct and to know that our kids would find their way in the world. Neither Cullen nor Gillian would fit into the rigid mold that others tried to force them into. Both are fun-loving and strong- willed. These attributes may play well in life but they did not always play well in the classroom. Like other things in life we must meet our children where they are and love them as they are, through all of their humanity and divinity.

So sure, maybe I was denying the reality of my situation. I am an ordinary woman, who loves my family and did not want to lose my husband. But I could justify being in denial by pointing to the fact that it allowed us to make the best of things. We did not spend too much time looking down the road. We lived in the present and did not waste those precious moments. In doing so, we connected one positive moment with the next one, and the next one, and pretty soon we had a pretty good day, a good week, a good month, a good year and a good life.

This journey, in spite of all the difficulties, was also providing us with spiritual vision and the ability to see through ordinary life into something deeper...and to live instead in the realm of the extraordinary.

Fred also planned a 40th birthday trip for me. We took the kids and traveled to the Grand Canyon and to California. We visited Fred's cousins in southern California, spent Easter in Santa Barbara, complete with a trip to the ocean as well as to the vineyards for some wine tasting.

When we were at the Grand Canyon, the comet, Hale Bopp, was making its way across the western sky and over the canyon. There was no light pollution there so we could see the comet clearly. One night we sat out at the canyon's rim and watched the stars come out and we marveled at the vastness of the universe.

I remember looking up at the night sky, in all of its grandeur and magnificence; Fred's body was warm as he wrapped his arms around me to keep the chill away. I was lost in my own thoughts as we sat in companionable silence. I don't know where the soul goes when it leaves the body but I know it goes somewhere. As I reflected on the vastness of the universe I realized how little I know about anything. I am suspect of people who think they have been granted the wisdom to know all things, or at least they act and speak as if they do.

In retrospect, when I look back on the photographs taken at the party and on the trip, I can see that Fred was thin and his color a bit ashen. His back was bothering him at the time. He did not think that he could hike very far down the canyon, but he encouraged me to take the kids for a hike into the canyon while he waited on the rim for us. When we returned, Fred was smiling and waiting to take our picture. I know he would not miss his opportunity to hike the canyon if he was able. He had back pain again. He did not complain and I repressed my worry and denied my concerns. We were not going to miss these beautiful days with our family.

As we headed home, I realized how we had changed and grown as individuals and as a couple. I learned over the years that he would self-regulate. I never pushed him to do more than he was up to. We were autonomous beings. We made our own decisions. He never got in the way of what I wanted to do and I offered him the same courtesy.

We really were equal partners. We did not feel the need to control one another as most of the time we lived in congruence and harmony and usually our first consideration was for the needs of one another and our children.

For all my preparation, I was not fully prepared for what lay ahead—either for the challenges or the miracles.

CHAPTER 12

The Edge of Eternity

Summer 1997

October 9, 1997 would be the 5th anniversary of Fred's bone marrow transplant. With multiple myeloma, if someone remains cancer free for 5 years after a BMT, they were considered cured. In my head I began to make plans for a celebration.

When school was out for summer we got ready to take the kids on what was now our annual camping trip to The Pinery with our friends from St. Hugo.

The morning before we went, Fred had his semi-annual bone marrow biopsy. The procedure is excruciating and still he voiced no complaints.

When we arrived at The Pinery most of the other families were already there. This year our entourage had grown to 8 families and 12 tents filled with adults and kids aged from 11 to 3 years old. The kids had just gotten out of school and were jumping out of their skin with the excitement of being on summer vacation and on the annual camping trip. The kids spent the days playing in the sand dunes and swimming in the ice-cold water, and the evenings were spent with a communal dinner, followed by a bonfire, roasted marshmallows and ghost stories until all the families retreated to their tents. The days' activities had worn out even the most energetic. The adults and the children crawled into their sleeping bags and welcomed sleep. When the sun went down it was cold but I was exhausted and fell asleep quickly.

I woke early in the morning. I was cold and the ground was hard in spite of the air mattress. It was early and the campground was still quiet. The sun was already up and was filtered through the mesh windows of the tent. I rolled over and surveyed the inside of the tent. The kids were nestled in and sleeping soundly but Fred was not in the tent. I pulled on a pair of jeans and my socks from the bottom of my bag and went to look for him. He had left silently sometime in the night and I found him sitting in the car. I climbed into the passenger seat, "Morning Honey." He leaned over to kiss me.

"Are you okay?" I asked.

"Sleeping on the ground is a little rough. I was cold and my back is a little sore." He acknowledged matter-of-factly but without complaint.

As I watched him, I thought, the BMT had left him with so many health issues. I tried not to over-think this or worry about him. He coped with his life each day as it presented itself. We had been walking this line between life and death for 7 years now. Was it possible that we had walked away from the dark ocean that tried to swallow Fred? Had we made it back inland to where everyone lives the kind of life where you don't always think about impending loss? I hoped so.

Almost immediately following the camping trip, we repacked the van, for our annual trip to visit my sister and her family on the Jersey shore. It was a wonderful week away but it was a long drive, and when we returned home everyone was exhausted. I needed to get the kids in the house and ready for bed without delay while Fred began to carry in the suitcases. I walked past the office and the light on the answering machine was blinking wildly. I made a mental note to check the messages after the kids were in bed. There were faces to wash, teeth to brush and clean pajamas to climb into. When I came downstairs, the light on the answering machine was no longer blinking.

Fred was sitting in the family room on the couch going through a stack of mail, sorting it into piles. "Who called? Anything important?" I asked as I sat down next to him and picked up my stack of mail.

He turned to face me and he nodded, "I had a message to call Dr. Jana. She called on Thursday."

I looked at him and mentally calculated the days. Today was Sunday so that was four days ago. "She called... herself?" I asked as I tried to weigh the importance of this news.

Fred nodded again. His face registered no emotion; "I'll call her in the morning."

It had been a long day. Thirteen hours in the car. We did not talk about this at the time or even speculate what it might mean but instead got cleaned up and ready for bed. We crawled into bed and fell asleep in one another's arms.

When I woke in the morning, Fred was already up and sitting at the kitchen counter. The newspaper was unopened and obviously unread on the counter and even though it was Monday, he was not dressed for work. "I called Dr. Jana." I looked at the clock. It was not yet 8 am. "The bone marrow biopsy…the results indicate an elevated level of IgG."

Fred's face was ashen and expressionless. We both understood the medical jargon and the implications all too well.

The myeloma had returned. The cancer was back.

I feel like I have been kicked in the stomach. My head spins and I fear I will collapse.

My brain is foggy about what happened next but I recall Fred saying, "I am so sorry." As if this was something he had willingly chosen. I am stunned with disbelief and incapacitated with emotional devastation. "This cannot be."

I am uncertain what happened next. My mind is befuddled and I am unable to recollect the happenings of the day. In retrospect, I now understand a little bit about the complexities of the human body and how Our Creator has lovingly designed us to cope with pain and tragedy. The adrenal glands produce cortisol to help us get through the crises in our lives, and it dulls the memory when things are too difficult for us to bear.

I have no idea what happened over the next couple of days. I think we probably retreated to the privacy of our bedroom as we attempted to shield the children from the reality of the situation. I am reasonably certain that we attempted to regroup before we faced our children and their myriad of questions that we were woefully unprepared to answer.

Cortisol is only a short-time protectant to get us through the immediate crisis, but this has been a marathon and I needed to rely on something else to cope. I know that I prayed relentlessly and begged God not to take my beloved. I was filled with terror.

Over the years that we had been on this journey we learned that the treatment can be as toxic as the cancer. When the malignancy returns following a bone marrow transplant, it often returns with a vengeance. Fred's doctors discussed his treatment options. The decision was made to start Fred back on chemotherapy.

Fred and I made plans to go away for the weekend, as we needed some time alone together. Before we left we had some family photos taken but by the end of the session Fred had developed a raging fever. I suggested we cancel the weekend and reschedule but Fred would not hear of it. Instead, he called his doctor and they ordered massive doses of antibiotics and antiviral medications that we picked up at the pharmacy on our way out of town.

We went to the Village of Chelsea for the weekend. Chelsea is a little town about 90 minutes from the house. We had dinner at the Common Grill and went to a play at the Purple Rose Theater. We stayed at a wonderfully romantic bed and breakfast.

Our candle lit room provided the peaceful backdrop for the passion that burned between us. We made love until we wept with ecstasy and relief and an uncontrollable sadness. How could this, which is so beautiful and so right, be coming to an end? Is it possible that people are allowed only so much happiness and we have already exceeded our quota? What in the name of God will I do without him? All I can do is hang on and love him while he is here. And so we had dried our tears and held on to one another and then we made love again, this time slowly and sweetly and we savored every moment and fell asleep entangled in one another's bodies.

All the while, I was so broken and he was so strong. On one level, we were as close as we had ever been, and on another I felt as if he was moving on ahead of me. He had accepted the path he was destined to walk and I was caught still fighting, kicking and screaming. "Please, please do not go without me." Our paths are beginning to diverge.

The dark and rough ocean of loss and fear crashed in at the shoreline of our lives . . . I really believed that our journey had taken us close to the edge of eternity, but that we had been fortunate enough to have avoided it and now we are here yet again.

Fall 1997

Fred was back on chemo and was getting good results. He was subjected to periodic bone marrow biopsies and thus we learned the malignant myeloma cells were decreasing. This was good news and we were grateful. Fred felt ill about one week each month following the chemotherapy, but the rest of the time he felt pretty well and we continued on with the business of living. We both knew that we were in a holding pattern, as Fred could not continue with the chemo indefinitely as it is toxic to his heart.

I realize that I was the one who struggled as we walked this very narrow line between this world and the next. I did not want to be here again and yet here we were.

I had been in denial of this reality for so long, as I tried my best to live in the present and not give away the precious moments of life by worrying about the future. Normal life had taken on an extraordinary quality and it did not stop because Fred was ill. Cullen was in fifth grade and Gillian was in second grade. I was in my second year of teaching at Detroit Country Day School and most days Fred was working, too. The kids went to latchkey after school and each afternoon I hurried to complete my work so I could take them home. Family time was sacrosanct.

While I struggled everyday to keep my heart from breaking, Fred was deepening into a peace I did not know.

In early December, Fred's doctor ordered some cardiac function tests and determined that he was unable to continue with the chemotherapy. He had crossed the threshold and any more chemo would be toxic to his heart; the chemo would lead to heart failure and if he continued, it would kill him. What now? The question loomed large. What else could be done?

Fred's doctor wanted to try a stem cell transplant from Kirk. In 1997, this type of transplant was considered cutting edge. Very few of this type of transplant had been done at the time. The risks and potential benefits were explained to us. It was proposed as Fred's only alternative. There isn't much to discuss when you have run out of options, so we gave our consent to try it.

The stem cell transplant was supposed to be similar to a second bone marrow transplant. It was scheduled for after Christmas. We did our best to live in the moment and tried not to look too far ahead but we both knew how brutal the first one had been. Fred would endure absolutely anything to stay with us but, Dear God, how much can one person take?

I would like to say that Fred and I discussed whether it would be better for him to refuse the second transplant, stop treatment and to submit to the will of God. But the truth is that I was totally unable and unwilling to broach that conversation with him. It was unfathomable. I was holding on to him with all the strength I could possibly muster. For me the question was: what will I do if I can't keep him? That path was a deep dark tunnel that I wanted no part of. I was afraid and I consciously chose not to look in that direction. I turned my back on the possibility, and true to my character I tried to keep to the sunny side.

Winter 1998
  The Stem Cell Transplant
  The theory behind a stem cell transplant is that Kirk's stem cells (known as the graft) will see Fred's malignant cells (the host) as foreign and attack them in an immune response. It was supposed to take 6 to 8 weeks for the graft to set up and attack the malignant cells. The science behind stem cell transplants was new. The doctors readily

admitted that they did not know the quantity of stem cells that needed to be harvested from Kirk and infused into Fred to be effective. This was all new at the time- we were dealing with best guesses and trial and error. The transfusion itself was successful and was the easy part for Fred. And then we waited. We monitored Fred daily for fever, a rash, or pain. According to the medical community these were supposed to be good signs that the transplant was working. We monitored. We waited. Months passed and nothing happened.

The year before, when our life had been on an even keel, we had made plans to go to Hilton Head with Shelley, Joel and the kids. Fred did not want to cancel the plans, just in case we could possibly go. Initially, he was insistent that the kids and I should go without him, but as the day we were supposed to leave approached, he asked me if I would stay home with him. I had wanted to stay with him all along. Perhaps he had a premonition and perhaps he was afraid that our time together was drawing towards the end. His fear terrified me, for throughout this whole ordeal he had been a pillar of strength, resilient and brave. What did he know that I was still unwilling to face?

April 1998

The doctors came to the conclusion that the stem cell transplant had not worked. They determined that they had not given enough stem cells and they wanted to try again. After the second infusion of Kirk's stem cells we were in the waiting mode again.

Fred was living at the edge of medical science and because of medical science, and I was at the edge of my faith. There are folks who believe that people live in two distinct worlds; those who put their faith in science and those who live in a spiritual realm. I believe it is the same realm. This journey has led me to believe that the more we understand the science, the closer we come to knowing Our Creator.

Science and spirituality converge. I read and wrote and prayed and loved and just held on.

We dared to hope and pray. I love Dr. Jana. She loves Fred and because of him she also cares for me. But this was new. We trusted that she had our best interests at heart. She is smart and loving.

This time they gave a much higher dose of Kirk's stem cells.

Fred got a response within days. He spent another Easter in the hospital. His white cell counts were dangerously low. Again, the kids were not allowed to visit him in the hospital for fear that they might be harboring an infection. We visited him through a glass window on Easter Sunday. He was the boy in the bubble. We could look at him but we could not touch him or get near him. His loneliness was palpable. We miss him and as always he put a good face on his situation in spite of everything.

May 1998

It was Gillian's First Communion. Fred went AWOL, absent without leave, from the hospital and sat in the back of the church wearing a surgical mask. He told me that he absolutely had to be there, for he feared that he might not be at her wedding. I know that his doctors had a fit, this was not in his best interest but

I understood his thinking. He made his own decisions and I supported him. He wanted to see his daughter make her First Communion.

She looked just like a little angel with her blond hair, translucent pink skin and her little white dress. She had been selected to be one of the readers during the Mass. She had a very difficult passage to read but she got through it and beamed with pride. During the homily, Monsignor Tony asked the children questions about Jesus. G sat in the front pew and she raised her little hand to answer all the questions. Her voice was strong and her answers illuminated an understanding that was well beyond her years.

Gillian's faith was simple and beautiful but in contrast, I continued to struggle with the unknown and the unknowable. My faith was being challenged. As I sat in the church, I realized that there were two forces still at odds in me. One force was the faith that I proclaimed to have, a faith in a God that loves me, and a belief that life continues beyond our earthly life. The other force I really struggled with, was the nagging question…why would a God that loves us allow so much suffering, and how will my life, and more importantly my children's lives, ever go on if Fred was taken from us? The suffering would be perpetuated.

There was evidence of graft versus host disease (GVHD). This was the intended outcome of the stem cell transplant: to have Kirk's stem cells attack Fred's malignant melanoma cells. The symptoms can be mild to severe and include abdominal pain, fever, jaundice, skin rash, vomiting, dry eyes, weight loss and lung disorders. This is supposed to be a good thing, as difficult as that is to believe. I needed to keep reminding myself of this but the reality was, it meant that my husband could not partake in the joys of everyday family life because he was too ill to be at home with the children.

First Communions are a big deal in our community of friends. Parties are given and friends and relatives are invited to help celebrate. We had a quiet celebration with an afternoon dinner at the house for our families and friends but Fred could not attend. Once again he was quarantined at his sister's, one house away. I brought him dinner on a plate. Gillian and Cullen accompanied me, and they had to peer in the windows to see their Dad and talk to him through the glass. They miss him.

Fred was put back on steroids to keep the GVHD at low levels. Steroids mask the symptoms, so they were mild. Once the GVHD was in check, Fred was allowed to move home, and we spent the summer at home and in the garden. Fred put the increased energy from the steroids to good use and decided to lay a natural slate patio that ran the length of the house under the wisteria-covered portico on the lake side of the house. Upon completion it was a beautiful work of art as these massive pieces of slate were pieced together like a puzzle.

Late in the summer, we traveled to northern Michigan for a week. We spent Gillian's 9th birthday on Drummond Island in Lake Huron. Fred gave Gillian a big girl bicycle for her birthday. It was a little bit too big for her but he was insistent that she get this bike for her birthday. He had taught her to ride a bike when she was a little girl and it was one of the many things that they loved to do together. In retrospect, perhaps he wanted her to think of him whenever she rode her bike and remember how much he loved her. She would ride this bike for years.

Early in the week we all rode our bikes around the island. But as the week progressed, I would kayak and bike with the kids, as Fred was too short of breath to participate. So instead he sat on the beach and watched patiently. He played putt-putt golf with the kids. We went on walks down the beach together, while the kids ran ahead and skipped stones into the lake. We even talked of buying some land in the Upper Peninsula.

All throughout our marriage we would day dream about where we would live when we retired and what we would do together when we were older, as if it was an absolute given and we would have all the time in the world to spend together.

By the end of the week Fred was becoming progressively shorter of breath. He was now too short of breath to lie flat when he slept. At my insistence, he called his doctor. His doctor thought the GVHD was attacking Fred's lungs and we were advised to cut the trip short and head for home immediately. Fred needed to be hospitalized and not just anywhere. He needed to be hospitalized where people had actually heard of GVHD and had an inkling of a clue what to do about it.

I was physically sick with fear. I could not eat, and if I tried I could not keep anything down . . . I lost weight. Fear set in and I was terrified.

Fred was in and out of the hospital. They increased his steroids and adjusted the multitude of medications yet again for the umpteenth time.

When we returned from vacation I made an appointment to have my haircut. I had been wearing it long for years but now the care it required had become far too time-consuming with all the chaos in my life. So in a spur of the moment decision I had it cut very short. I returned to school ten pounds lighter and with short hair. My colleagues commented on how good I looked.

Great, it was the stress diet. People assumed that all was well and I did nothing to disturb their illusions. However, in reality I was just barely functional. I could not eat because I was afraid. I could not sleep. I used exercise to try to control what could not be controlled. I was just barely putting one foot in front of the other as I tried to stay present, and in the now.

Fred's words haunted me. "Don't mourn me while I am here." I did my best to abide by his wishes, but it was so hard, so damn hard. I am not a stupid woman. The life that I knew and loved was unraveling and I was ill-prepared.

Fred's friends from college came to visit over the Labor Day weekend. They had purchased tickets to go to the Tigers' Game. Fred wanted to see them but already he was very short of breath. He needed to stop frequently to rest and catch his breath as they walked through the stadium. I cooked and we had a barbeque by the lake. His friends all brought sleeping bags and they camped out all over our house. They love him and they would travel to the ends of the earth to tell him so, and they did.

So we found ourselves at the end of the summer— also nearing the end of our options.

Fred's health was deteriorating rapidly; by the end of the next week he needed to use a wheelchair and was on oxygen, as he became so short of breath with any exertion at all.

Fred was going to the hospital daily as his doctors tried to control the GVHD. When he was not at the hospital he still went to the office, even in the wheel chair and with the oxygen. He persisted in attending to the needs of the day. He was unwilling to let go of anything.

I am again reminded of his words to me, "We will not speak of dying. There is living and there is dead. As long as I am here, I am living." We went to Cullen's soccer games and had dinner together at home every evening with our family.

September 19, 1998

Fred called me at work and told me, "Honey, they are going to hospitalize me again. I'm sorry." He had a high fever, pneumonia and was short of breath. It was GVHD and pneumonia. Kirk's stem cells continued to attack Fred's lungs. In response his lungs were becoming scarred and fibrous. His breathing was becoming ineffective and his lungs were filling with fluid. "They are going to try to reverse the immune response with massive doses of steroids."

I close the door to my office. I cry. My heart is breaking. I have been in denial for so long. I have ferociously clung to my beloved. He is so sick. I am terrified. I am still bargaining with God but I feel as if I have played all the cards in my hand. I have nothing left to offer up. I am broken and depleted.

I visit Fred every day. I go to the hospital between classes, when my schedule allows, to bring him his favorite foods and to bathe him. He is so short of breath. Everything tires him out. He is losing weight. When I cannot go during the day, I go as soon as school is over.

One day after school when I arrive at the hospital, Dr. Jana is waiting for me at the nurse's station. She takes me down a hall to a private consultation room and closes the door. She sits beside me on the couch and holds my hand and looks in my eyes. This is not good...what has happened? . . . I just spoke with him 30 minutes ago. I try to be present.

"Jeanne, this is so hard." She pauses a moment to collect herself. "I have already spoken with Fred. As I am sure you know, the steroids are no longer working. I am afraid that I am out of options." There are tears rolling freely down her face and mine too. I hold my breath and keep silent. "It is time to take Fred home. It is time to call hospice. I have nothing more to offer him. He is such a wonderful man. I am so very sorry."

Once again, I feel myself stepping away from this moment—from this world.

I feel like my heart is being ripped from my chest. My heart feels like it is tearing.

"This cannot be." I cry out in anguish and despair. But in my heart I know that she speaks the truth. As much as I have tried to deny this reality, I am not a stupid woman and I know that the time is near. Dr. Jana is gentle and kind as she patiently sits with me while I sob, but in the end the message is the same.

We are out of time. The person I need now is Fred and only Fred.

Fred is in his hospital room, sitting up in the bed. He looks at me with tears in his eyes and gives me a beautiful smile. As I approach him he moves over to make a place for me and pats the bed beside him and I climb into the bed with him. We do not speak. Sometimes words are just so inadequate. He holds me while we cry until we both fall asleep.

The sun is setting over the city when we wake. Fred says, "I think we need to talk about the hard stuff."

"Okay, honey," and the tears start all over again. We have had these conversations before but not often.

We discuss the children. "I so wanted to be here to see them grown. You have been a wonderful wife and mother. You are the greatest of all my life's blessings. "

I am so broken up that I cannot respond. And so he continues, "I know that you will continue to be a wonderful mother and will make decisions with the kids' best interests at heart. Just trust your heart and know that I am with you."

He takes a minute to catch his breath and I wait. He has things he needs to tell me and I sit with him in silence as I wait for him to continue. " I do not want Cullen to go to the Christian Brothers for high school, too many assholes come out of that school. I know you will find a way to nurture the Renaissance man that Cullen is . . . athletic, academic and artistic."

He moves on to Gillian, "Our dear little Gillian, she is my late blooming flower." I begin to cry again as I can see that his heart is breaking. "You must continue to nurture her gentle spirit with patience and tenderness. Do not allow anyone to push her to be like all the other flowers in the garden. Remember that some flowers bloom in the spring and some bloom in the fall. Allow her to blossom as she is supposed to."

I need to catch my breath. I get out of the bed and walk about the room. I take a few slow deep breaths. I need a moment, just a moment to process what is happening here. Then I pull a chair up next to the bed so that I can see his beautiful face. We hold one another's hands. His speech is somewhat halting as he struggles to breathe. We discuss burial versus cremation. "I think you should have my body buried. I know that cremation would be hard for your mother. I love her so much, she has been so good to me and I don't want to inflict any more pain on her. But no open casket."

I give him my word.

We talk about which cemetery for the burial and decide on the cemetery in town, not the Catholic cemetery. His family plot in Port Huron is full. "I think we should have a burial plot for Shelley, Joel and Kirk as well as your Mom and Dad." He worries that I will drive by the cemetery everyday as it is on the outskirts of town. "I don't want you to think of me every time you drive by the cemetery."

"My darling, I will think of you always." I tell him and I break down and begin to cry all over again. He has planned this conversation very carefully and has thought about what is best for all of us that he will leave behind.

Then it was my turn...Fred wanted me to face my future without him. "If one of us should pass before the other, I want you to know that it is okay with me if you look for love again. I want you to. But I want you to look for a best friend. Trust me, there are lots of men who would love to be with you. But I know you, and you, my dear, need a best friend." All I can do is nod and acknowledge that I hear what he is saying as I cannot begin to see my life without him, let alone a life with someone else. The tears run freely down my face and I make no attempt to stop them or wipe them away.

We talk about his passing. In my brokenness I say, "It may be decades and decades before I pass. I have a lot of longevity in my family. What if I move? No doubt I will change . . . I may be a very old woman." I finally give words to my worries about his going on before me.

He reassures me, "Please don't worry, sweetheart; when the time arrives I will come for you. I will know you anywhere. Souls are ageless and yours is so beautiful."

October 2, 1998

I brought Fred home from the hospital. I know that he wanted me to be ready but I could only deal with this a little at a time. I was not in control and never had been. I tried to manage the tangible details of my life, and most of the time that was all I was capable of.

I called the family and they rallied. They were at our beck and call. No need, no matter how minor, went unanswered. I do not know how I got through these days; the truth is that I was carried by the love and mercy of these angels that I am blessed to call my family.

I made arrangements with Brad, my boss, for a leave of absence and I broke down and cried in his office. He is a good-hearted man and he tried to be reassuring, "Fred has rallied before."

I told him, "This time is different." No more pretending. I could no longer afford the luxury of denial. He told me to take as much time as I needed and he hired two people to do my job.

People called and began to arrive uninvited. They needed to tell Fred how much he meant to them. Robin Nance drove down from Traverse City. Her three-year-old son died a few years ago. She asked Fred to be a messenger of her love to her son, Evan. He assured her that he would. We all cried. It wore him out. I needed to protect him.

The next night our dear friend and neighbor, Laurie Stern stopped by and she was delusional with grief. She could not stay; it was too hard on Fred.

Arlene Rama and her partner, Linda, brought a carload full of food to the house from all my colleagues at Country Day. They did not stay to visit with Fred, as it was too difficult for him to speak and breathe.

The next afternoon, Ed Duke came to the house. Fred and Ed had been friends since law school and we are the Godparents to his three children. They love each other. Ed was at a loss for words and Fred was struggling to breathe. Their visit was short. When Ed left, Fred whispered to me, "no more."

Shelley, Joel, and Kirk stayed with us at the house. When Fred was awake we sat with him and watched movies, laughed and rubbed his feet and shoulders. He slept off and on in a recliner, as he was way too short of breath to lie down. And now to complicate matters further, Fred had begun to cough up blood.

October 7,1998

In the morning, Fred asked me to call his lawyer. I had never heard of a lawyer that made house calls. But Tom did, or at least he did for Fred. I bathed Fred. It was important to him to be presentable when Tom arrived. In the midst of this unfolding tragedy, Fred and I shared an intimate moment.

Later Tom Bergh arrived and all the papers were signed. Fred was abundantly clear about which assets were to go into which trusts, and the trusts had been tightly drawn according to his will. He made certain that his family was well taken care of.

When this last order of business was completed he told me, "I think it is time to call hospice."

The hospice nurse arrived and did a lengthy assessment and ordered a hospital bed. She told Fred he did not need to worry about bathing daily. He looked over at me and gave me a sly smile and all I could do was laugh and shake my head at him. She caught the drift and told him that on the other hand he certainly could bathe as often as he liked. The hospice nurse made plans to return the next morning. She knew better than to try to predict the future. I am a nurse and I have seen many people at death's door. My heart knew that it would not be long now. Fred was still mentally clear but he was struggling to breathe. He could not go on like this for long.

The Union, our favorite local restaurant sent over dinner. The word was out and our entire community knew that the end was near. Fred could hardly swallow. He could not eat. His breathing was labored. He was coughing up blood. He slept in the chair as he could not lie down and breathe. His lungs were filling up with fluid. I slept on the couch in the family room so I could be near if he needed anything. Shelley, Joel, Kirk and the kids all stay close.

October 8, 1998

On the way to school the next morning, I tell the children that their Daddy is dying. They cry. They are angry. They tell me not to say that. We talk of heaven and of God's promises and of a life beyond this earthly one.

Gillian's class is helping on the altar today. She wants me to stay for Mass. I stay because she is so sad and afraid and she needs me too. The priest, Father Bob, follows me out of church. "I understand that your husband is very sick. Would you like me to visit today?" I thank him but say no. Our parish priest visited last week and did the final anointing. I just want to get home. I know that time is short and I want to be with my husband.

Later that morning, the hospital bed arrives and we set it up in the family room. The hospice nurse arrives with morphine. She gives Fred some under his tongue and his breathing eases a little. He wants to go out on the deck. It is a beautiful fall day. It is still warm, the day is clear and the sun is shining. Fred wants to see the last roses of the season in his garden. He is outside for a few minutes and then he lets us know that he is ready to be wheeled back into the house. Joel and Kirk lift him out of the wheelchair and into the recliner where he sleeps off and on all afternoon.

Mom and Dad call from Europe. Fred and I had been insistent that they go, as they had planned this trip long ago, but now it is time for them to come home. When they left, two weeks ago, we all thought that we would have many more days with Fred when they returned; I know differently now.

Friends bring our children home from their afterschool activities. Shelley, Joel and Kirk are with us. Freddy wakes up and is completely alert and the kids and I sit on an ottoman at his feet. We all sit close to him. He smiles at us and his face glows with a beautiful radiance.

He smiles at the kids and starts to move his neck. The kids recognize what he is doing immediately. They laugh and call out, "Dad's doing the turkey neck dance!" He nods and smiles. He does this for the kids. Dancing was one of the many things that they always did together.

Fred begins to look up towards the ceiling and speaks to people that we cannot see. There is no fear on his face. He is smiling and joyful. I have seen this before. This was how it was when Gram was speaking with Blanche just days before she died. I know that there are spirits in the room with us. Fred knows them and he is not afraid. His face radiates with delight. They have come to help him cross over. I absolutely know this to be true.

Fred turns his gaze towards us and looks at each of us individually and with absolute clarity he says in the most poignant way, "I love you all," and then he turns his gaze towards the heavens and says, "Power Up."

He smiles at us for the last time and then slips into a coma.

We sit with him a while and no one speaks. We are awestruck, as we have just witnessed a miracle.

It is a fallacy that we have been told that we come into this world alone and that we go out of it alone. Freddy has been loved every day of his life. Now those who have loved him and have gone on before him have come back. They are here to help him with the crossing over. He is not afraid and I take enormous comfort in what I have just witnessed.

Within a short period of time, Joel and Kirk carry him to the hospital bed. We take turns sitting up with him, while others take shifts sleeping on the couch. Fred's breathing is shallow and labored. In the early morning I hold his hand and pray the Rosary. Fred and I and the kids have long prayed an alternative Hail Mary. Fred learned this version from Father Farrell and I know he likes it.

Hail Mary full of grace
The Lord is with you
Blessed are you among women
And blessed is the fruit of thy womb, Jesus
Holy Mary Mother of God
*Pray for us **children***
*Now and at the hour of our **birth***
Amen

As I pray the rosary, Freddy breathes his last.
It is 7:10 am.
October 9, 1998.
Freddy passes on to eternity.

I clean his body.
It is cold.
This life has passed out of his body slowly.
Suddenly, I feel his presence in the room.
He waits with me and watches as I wash his body and wrap it in a warm blanket.

I know now that the promises made about life after death are not just empty words. I know that life does go on. The body dies but the spirit leaves the body and the spirit is eternal.

This life has challenged me in ways I did not know I was capable of enduring but please do not pity me or cry for me because I have also been greatly blessed. I have loved and been loved and I know beyond all telling that I will be with Fred again.

Take my hand and lead me to salvation
Take my love
for love is everlasting
and remember
the truth that once was spoken
to love another person
is to see the face of God
    – Victor Hugo
    Les Miserables

231

CHAPTER 13

Epilogue

The newspapers carried stories about Fred's passing. One story was entitled, <u>Fred's Death, in the end, was a Lesson in Living.</u> The story goes on to say that, "Fred Miller was about the bravest and nicest guy I've ever known." He was described as the man with the dulcet tones, as his voice was always pleasant and sweet. Fred was quoted as saying that, "you do not sit around and mope when time is short." The Oakland Press went on to say, "His is a legacy of courage, compassion and caring. His passionate devotion to his family turned a three-month death sentence into seven years of life, which he graciously shared with us. Fred Miller was an amazing spirit who, while dying, showed us all how to live."

And another article was entitled, <u>Lawyer Remembered for Strength and Kindness</u>. Judge Mester was quoted, "He had the tenaciousness of a good prosecutor and the compassion of a good human being. He recognized that the primary pursuit of justice was to follow the law, but to couple justice with mercy. This is a very sad moment." Fred's boss Richard Thompson described Fred as "inspirational." And another attorney said, "Fred was an outstanding trial attorney who had a great way with juries. His integrity and honesty came through. He wore it like a second skin."

This was a part of Fred's life that I only saw glimpses of when he was home. The County Executive and former prosecutor, L. Brooks Patterson said, "He was one of the best trial lawyers we had. He didn't beat his own drum." And that was true. It was very apparent to me, that the children and I were not the only ones who loved him and were blessed to have known him.

Fred's funeral Mass was a celebration of his life. Father William Murphy celebrated the Mass and during the homily he told Fred stories that made everyone laugh and cry. Father Murphy wanted people to know that he felt he was Fred's Father in the Faith. And rightly so, as Father Murphy was one of Fred's spiritual guides.

Hundreds and hundreds of people came to the funeral home and to the funeral Mass. They came from all over and each had a story to tell about how their lives had been made better in some way by their encounters with Fred. The eulogizing had gone on for well over two hours when our parish priest thought it was best if we proceed to the cemetery for the burial.

The sun shone brightly in the mid-day sky. It was unseasonably beautiful for October as the bagpiper played "Amazing Grace" and Fred's body was laid to rest. All in all, it had been a beautiful celebration of a life well-lived.

One afternoon, in the days that followed the funeral, I was alone in the car. I was driving near The Academy of the Sacred Heart, where Gillian would eventually go to high school. The sunlight was coming through the colored fall leaves on the maple trees and the interior of the car was basked in a beautiful warmth and golden light, and in that moment I felt Fred's presence in the light. I was comforted by his loving presence. It lasted only a matter of minutes, but that time hangs in my memory and I believe that he was with me.

In the weeks and months to follow, the light would go out for me, and the cold wet grey of late autumn would encase my being, and pervasive loneliness was my constant companion. Friends and loved ones got on with the business of living and the expectation was that we would do the same.

But I had been blessed with a good reason to drag my bones from bed, even when I would rather not. I would put a good face on the day because Cullen and Gillian needed me and I needed them. So I tried to be strong and cheerful because I know that Fred expected nothing less of me and because I was bound and determined not give up on this life that I have been given.

But when I would go to bed alone every night, my last thought would be that Fred was gone, and it would be my first thought upon waking. Often that waking would be in the early morning hours, and it was then that I felt most alone as I waited for dawn and a reason to get up and try again. I remember thinking: will it always be like this? I now know that time heals, even the large gaping wounds of the heart.

During that first fall and into the early winter there was a light that graced my bedroom ceiling in the evenings. The light was in the shape of a bird; I saw it as a dove. I had seen it a few times and thought it was peculiar and I looked for a reasonable explanation but I could not find a source for the light. One night when Gilly could not sleep she came downstairs and climbed in bed with me. Without any prompting from me, she said, "Look Mommy, Daddy has come to see us." She saw clearly that which I was skeptical of, and I believe she was right. Fred's spirit was visiting and he stayed with us for a few weeks and then one day the light was no longer visible. I can only report that which I have seen.

In the years that followed, I had plenty of time to reflect on my journey with Fred and all that I had been blessed to learn along the way.

Clearly Fred would have qualified as one of Dr. Bernie Siegel's exceptional cancer patients, as he lived far longer than he was expected to live, and there is a lesson in that. But more importantly Siegel says, "Success and healing refer to what you do with your life, not how long you avoid death."

Fred's boss and dear friend, Ron Covault, gave the eulogy at Fred's funeral. He said, "Fred lived and accomplished more in his 48 years while he was ill than most people accomplish in a lifetime while they are well." In walking the line between his humanity and his divinity, Fred was an accomplished human being. He was well loved by all who knew him but the value of his life was not found in the extensive list of his accomplishments.

Fred was exceptional because of the way he lived his life. Father Edward Farrell taught that each of us is an individual facet of God's glory. Fred lived his life in such a way that he radiated the divine spirit of God that resided within him. For Fred, love was a verb. He was a clear channel of love and goodness.

The first year after Fred died was difficult as well as beautiful, as the kids and I bound together and learned to operate as a threesome. Fred had taught us to be strong and so we were. I probably indulged the kids more than I should have but I wanted to expose them to some of the grandeur of life. So over the years we traveled to Mexico, Hawaii, to Yellowstone and the Grand Tetons, to the Caribbean and took multiple ski trips to the Rockies. They fell in love with life and all of its diversity, and I know their Dad approves, even if the well-intentioned voiced their objections. The kids and I were making it up as we went along and we had a lot of fun along the way. Death had taught us to seek out the golden treads of this very precious life we have been given and not to waste our days.

My children and I have a habit of speaking of their Dad like he is sitting in the next room. I know this makes some people uncomfortable, as they have very freely told me so. But the kids had been with him when he died and they know that his spirit resides just beyond the veil.

During one of the eulogies, a friend of Fred's recounted a story of how Fred would stop and have an ice cream cone everyday in the summer on his way back to the office after lunch. He could get away with this indulgence as he was tall and lean but she saw this as a special part of his character as he enjoyed and appreciated the little things in life. She challenged everyone at the funeral to find the little joys in their daily lives. She left the pulpit saying, "Have a Fred Miller day."

This became one of our family's mantras as we looked for and found everyday joy in our lives.

Fred taught me to partake in the richness of life. He came into my life and passed through my life as my lover, my husband, my friend and the father of my children. He was and is a channel of the Divine Spirit. He taught me how to live in the face of mortality. We had an external life of this world, which I clung to with all that was in me, but we also had an internal life of the spirit.

Someone once compared our spirits to paired skaters, and in the end his spirit has gone on without me and now I skate alone.

I vacillate between days of faith, hope and love and days of fear: fear of the pain of missing you, fear of solitude, fear that no one will ever know me again, fear of loneliness and fear of losing my way. And then there are days of faith, hope and love: faith that you are just *a breath away*, hope upon hope that you will indeed come for me when my time comes, and the promise that a loving God would not keep you and I apart eternally.

I struggle. Some days are easier than others.

It is difficult to be on a spiritual journey because when we are of this world we walk a path that weaves between our humanity and our divinity. Some days we walk in the light and we are spirit led, and other days our humanity and our very human needs and desires take us far afield from our spiritual journey. The beautiful thing is that this life we have been given is for practice, and every day is a new day to practice: love, generosity, repentance and forgiveness.

It has been almost fourteen years since Fred left this world and not a day goes by that I don't think of him and thank God for sending him to me, albeit too brief. It is helpful to see my children flourish. Cullen is now a musician in San Francisco and he works in the arts. He has known for a long time that he is on a spiritual journey. I often seek his guidance as we explore what we know and what we don't know about the Divine. He is truly the Renaissance Man that his father had hoped he would become. He is smart, well read, creative, athletic, loving and kind. I am truly blessed to know him, let alone have him as my son.

Gillian is a student at the University of British Columbia and she has blossomed into the bright and beautiful woman that God has created her to be. She is open hearted and a spiritual compass. She shows me the way. She lives to serve humanity, she treats all of God's creatures with love and compassion and tireless energy.

I believe there is a Divine Plan and that Our Creator in his or her infinite wisdom chose these children to help me to see the beauty and fulfillment of God's grace in my life. I live in the now, and revel in the blessings of the day.

I have learned much as I live on the edge of eternity. I look to see the presence of God in all living things. I have learned that the only moment we have is this one right now. See it for the beautiful gift it is and do not waste it for you will not get it back. Value every moment of your life, for if you believe in a life after this one and that the soul is eternal, then you are living in eternity right now.

There is an old adage that says that we come into this world alone and we go out of this world alone. The underlying assumption is that the only person you can really rely on is yourself. Upon reflection, this is untrue. It is a fallacy. The veil between this physical world and the spiritual world is very thin; for all of us, the spiritual world is only *a breath away*. At the time of our passing, those whom we have loved, who have gone on before us, will come back for us. We do not die alone. I have witnessed this. Not once but twice. Do not be afraid, someone waits beyond the veil.

∽

The soundtrack to my life plays on:

The Promise

If you wait for me
then I'll come for you
Although I've traveled far
I always hold a place for you in my heart

If you think of me
If you miss me once in awhile
Then I'll return to you
I'll return and fill that space in your heart

Remembering
Your touch
Your kiss
Your warm embrace
I'll find my way back to you
If you'll be waiting
If you dream of me like I dream of you
In a place that's warm and dark
In a place where I can feel the beating of your heart

Remembering
Your touch
Your kiss
Your warm embrace
I'll find my way back to you
If you'll be waiting
I've longed for you and I have desired
To see your face your smile
To be with you wherever you are

Remembering
Your touch
Your kiss
Your warm embrace
I'll find my way back to you
Please say you'll be waiting

Together again
It would feel so good to be
In your arms
Where all my journeys end
If you can make a promise
If it's one that you can keep
I vow to come for you
If you wait for me and say you'll hold
A place for me in your heart
   – Tracy Chapman

I try to be present in my own life and to live with gratitude that I live in the Grace of God. What is grace but unmerited kindness and mercy. I have been blessed to know real love. Life has blessed me abundantly. I live on in gratitude for I know that the days of this life are numbered. It is a time-limited gift. I still have things I need to learn and I intend to be present to do so.

I know beyond all telling
that on the other side of the veil . . .
just *a breath away* . . .
someone waits for me.

16690533R00144

Made in the USA
Charleston, SC
06 January 2013